THE *Chocolate* COOKBOOK

THE Chocolate COOKBOOK

Deliciously decadent recipes for cakes, tarts, cookies and sauces

Photography William Reavell

APPLE

First published in the UK in 2005 by Apple Press
4th Floor
Sheridan House
114 Western Road
Hove BN3 1DD
www.apple-press.com

ISBN 1-84543-078-6

Originally published in Italy as "An Inordinate Fondness for Chocolate"
This book was conceived, edited and designed by McRae Books Srl

Borgo santa Croce, 8 – 50122 Florence, Italy

www.mcraebooks.com

Publishers: Anne McRae and Marco Nardi
Project Director: Anne McRae
Design Director: Sara Mathews
Text by the Editors of McRae Books Srl.
Editing: Helen Farrell
Photography: William Reavell
Food Stylist: Tonia George
Stylist: Penny Markham
Colour separations: Fotolito Toscana

Printed in Italy

10 9 8 7 6 5 4 3 2 1

Contents

Introduction

"If any man has drunk a little too deeply from the cup of physical pleasure; if he has spent too much time at his desk that should have been spent asleep; if his fine spirits have become temporarily dulled; if he finds the air too damp, the minutes too slow, and the atmosphere too heavy to withstand; if he is obsessed by a fixed idea which bars him from any freedom of thought: if he is any of these poor creatures, we say, let him be given a good pint of amber-flavored chocolate....and marvels will be performed."
Anthelme Brillat-Savarin (1755–1826)

Chocolate doesn't grow on trees! Well, actually, it does, or at least the cacao beans from which it is made do. And the trees are so very aptly named — *Theobroma cacao* — which means "food of the gods." Despite the most obvious modern interpretation of this name, it was given to the plant by the Swedish naturalist Linnaeus with reference to an Aztec myth about Quetzalcoatl who stole a cacao tree from his fellow gods in paradise. He took the beans to earth, traveling on a beam of the morning star, and gave them to the people of Mexico. Quetzalcoatl also taught the women how to roast and grind the beans to make a nourishing paste that could be dissolved in water. The first Europeans in Central America seemed to confirm this tale when they described female vendors who made and sold "the drink of nobles" infused with chili water, flowers, vanilla, and honey.

Processing cacao beans into an edible substance is a fairly complicated business, and the method seems to have been discovered by the Olmecs whose complex civilization arose in the humid lowlands of the Mexican Gulf Coast about 3,500 years ago. They passed this skill onto the Mayas who succeeded them and who, in turn, are thought to have transferred the knowledge north, to the Aztecs.

For all the peoples of Mesoamerica, chocolate was far more than just the main ingredient in many delicious drinks, as well as gruels, porridges, and powders. It was deeply entwined with their culture and daily life, so much so that cacao beans were widely used as small currency to acquire items used in housekeeping or to pay laborers. There were also festivals and feast days to celebrate the gods associated with growing, harvesting, and processing cacao beans. The use of chocolate was mandatory at all celebrations and ceremonies, especially among the wealthy.

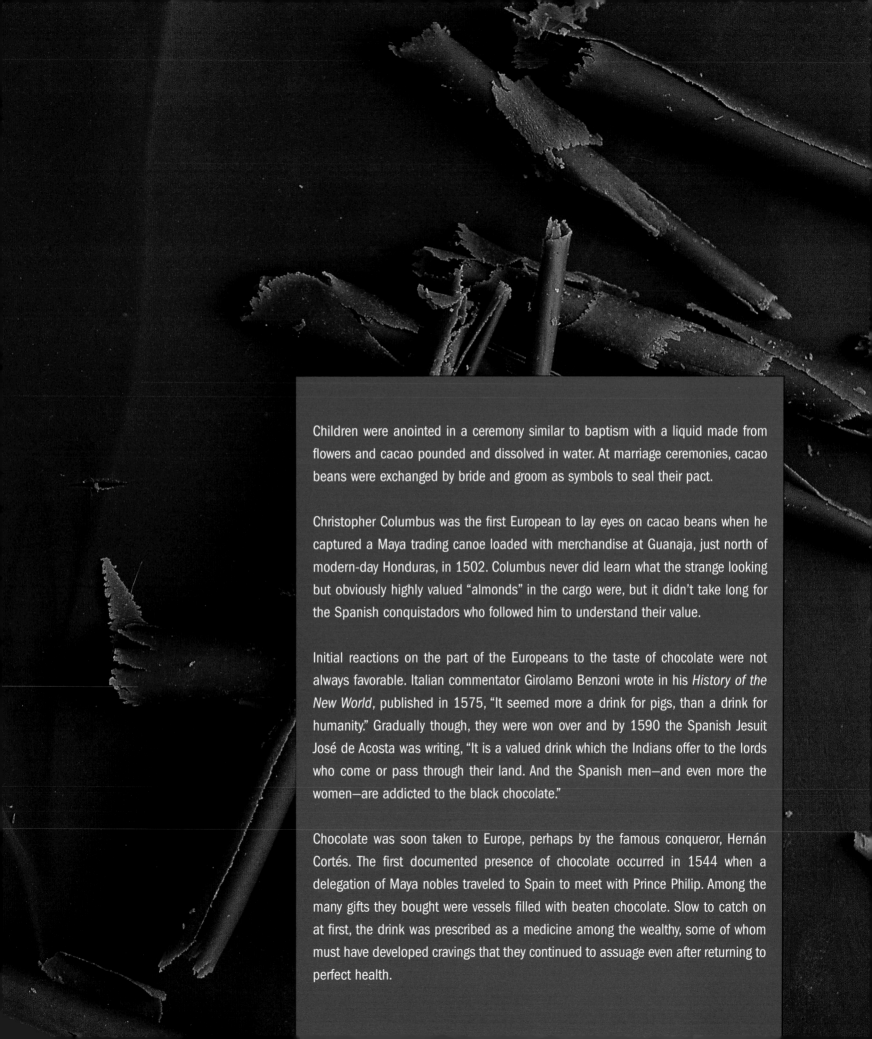

Children were anointed in a ceremony similar to baptism with a liquid made from flowers and cacao pounded and dissolved in water. At marriage ceremonies, cacao beans were exchanged by bride and groom as symbols to seal their pact.

Christopher Columbus was the first European to lay eyes on cacao beans when he captured a Maya trading canoe loaded with merchandise at Guanaja, just north of modern-day Honduras, in 1502. Columbus never did learn what the strange looking but obviously highly valued "almonds" in the cargo were, but it didn't take long for the Spanish conquistadors who followed him to understand their value.

Initial reactions on the part of the Europeans to the taste of chocolate were not always favorable. Italian commentator Girolamo Benzoni wrote in his *History of the New World*, published in 1575, "It seemed more a drink for pigs, than a drink for humanity." Gradually though, they were won over and by 1590 the Spanish Jesuit José de Acosta was writing, "It is a valued drink which the Indians offer to the lords who come or pass through their land. And the Spanish men—and even more the women—are addicted to the black chocolate."

Chocolate was soon taken to Europe, perhaps by the famous conqueror, Hernán Cortés. The first documented presence of chocolate occurred in 1544 when a delegation of Maya nobles traveled to Spain to meet with Prince Philip. Among the many gifts they bought were vessels filled with beaten chocolate. Slow to catch on at first, the drink was prescribed as a medicine among the wealthy, some of whom must have developed cravings that they continued to assuage even after returning to perfect health.

And so chocolate spread from Spain to Italy, France, and the rest of Europe. It journeyed with two other new drinks destined to become enormously popular—coffee and tea. Coffee-houses were established where an array of drinks were served, including hot chocolate. Even so, chocolate long remained an elite drink, a beverage for the discerning and well-off.

At this time too, chefs began to experiment with chocolate as a flavoring for sauces and other foods. In northern Italy, especially, cooks were exploring the possibilities of chocolate not only in cakes and other sweet preparations, but also in pasta and meat dishes. Our recipes for *Chocolate fettuccine with butter, sage, and mozzarella*, *Gnocchi with golden raisins and cocoa*, and *Venetian ravioli* (see pages 30 and 32) are part of this Italian tradition. Mesoamerican cooks did not use chocolate in their cooking and even though the *mole* is considered a classic of Mexican cuisine, it was not invented until the 17th century. There is some dispute as to whether the Italians were not the first to make use of chocolate in cooking.

Today the word chocolate conjures up a delectable bar of solid, sweet, and probably milky substance; this is a fairly recent innovation, dating to the Industrial Revolution. In this book we have tried to link this modern idea of chocolate to its origins by choosing a broad spectrum of recipes, ranging from those in the first two chapters for drinks and savory dishes, to the more usual offerings of cakes, cookies, pies, candies, desserts, and sauces in the remaining chapters. Although even here, you will find some intriguing ideas—try, for example, the *Eggplant with chocolate* in the desserts chapter (see page 110). We hope you will enjoy preparing these recipes as much as we have delighted in their preparation.

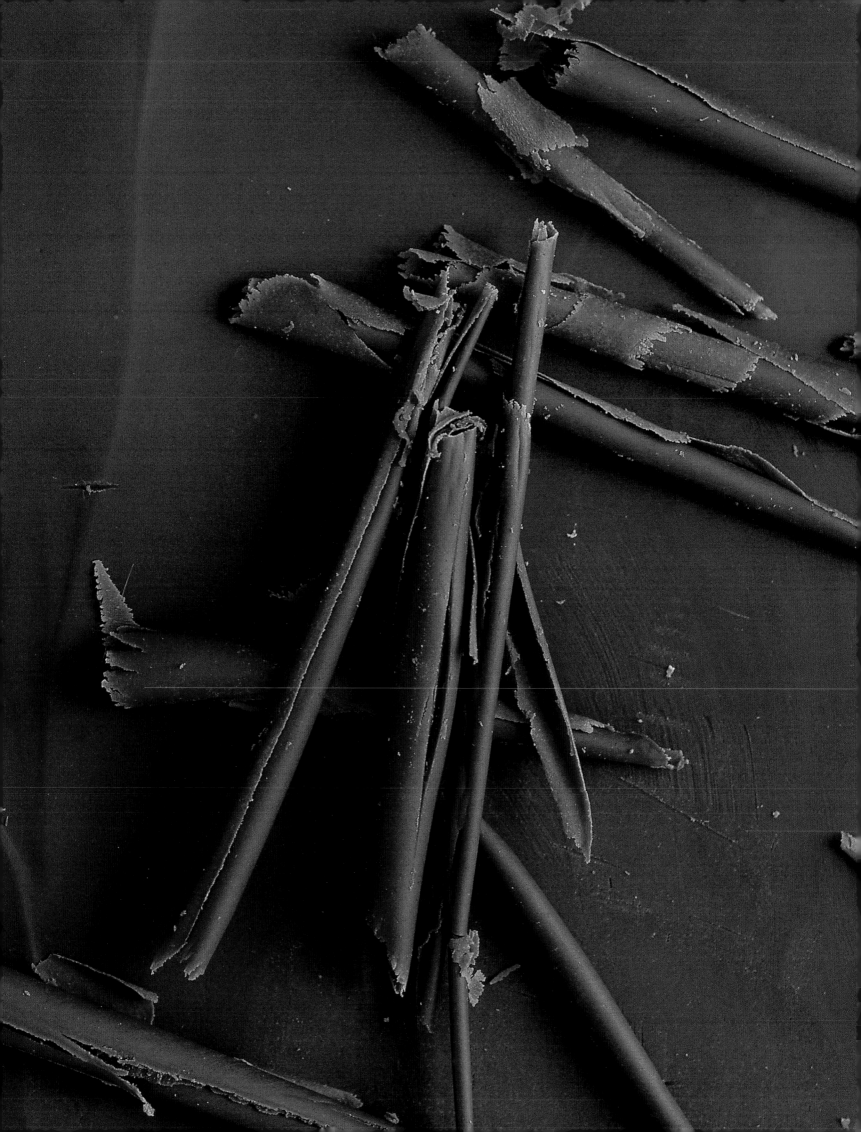

Drinks

"The divine drink which builds up resistance and fights fatigue.
A cup of this precious drink permits a man to walk for
a whole day without food."
Hernán Cortés (1485–1547)

chocolate cherry vodka martini

Serves 1 | Prep: 5 min | Level: 1

4 tablespoons (60 ml) chocolate-flavored
    liqueur
4 tablespoons (60 ml) cherry wine
4 tablespoons (60 ml) vodka
1 tablespoon (15 ml) chocolate syrup
Fresh cherries and chocolate-dipped cherries,
    to garnish

Classy and irresistible.

Fill a cocktail shaker with ice. | Add the chocolate and cherry liqueurs and vodka. | Shake briskly to mix and chill. | Drizzle the chocolate syrup into a chilled martini glass and strain in the cocktail. | Garnish with the cherries.

chocolate hazelnut vodka martini

Serves 1 | Prep: 5 min | Level: 1

2 tablespoons (30 ml) vodka
1 tablespoon (15 ml) hazelnut liqueur
1 tablespoon (15 ml) crème de cacao

Substitute the hazelnut liqueur with almond, orange, or mint liqueur for a dramatic change of flavor.

Fill a cocktail shaker with ice. | Add the vodka, hazelnut liqueur, and crème de cacao. | Shake briskly to mix and chill. | Strain the cocktail into a chilled martini glass.

dark russian

Serves 1 | Prep: 5 min | Level: 1

2 scoops chocolate ice cream
4 tablespoons (60 ml) milk
2 tablespoons (30 ml) dark crème de cacao
2 tablespoons (30 ml) cinnamon schnapps
2 tablespoons (30 ml) vodka
Slices of fresh banana, to garnish

Blend all the ingredients (except the banana) in a blender until smooth. You may have to pulse on and off until the mixture starts to swirl. | Pour the cocktail into a chilled highball or collins glass. Garnish with the slices of banana.

brandy alexander

Serves 1 | Prep: 5 min | Level: 1

3 tablespoons (45 ml) brandy
3 tablespoons (45 ml) light (single) cream
2 tablespoons white crème de cacao
Freshly grated nutmeg, to dust

Fill a cocktail shaker with ice. | Add the brandy, cream, and crème de cacao. Shake well and strain into a chilled martini glass. | Dust with the nutmeg.

mint chocolate ice-cream cocktail

Serves 1 | Prep: 5 min | Level: 1

4 tablespoons (60 ml) green crème de menthe
  (green mint liqueur)
2 scoops chocolate ice cream
Dash of milk to taste
Mint leaves, to garnish

Blend the crème de menthe and ice cream in a blender until smooth. | Add enough milk to make the cocktail creamy and drinkable. | Pour into a chilled old fashioned glass and garnish with the mint.

a taste of the caribbean

Serves 1 | Prep: 5 min | Level: 1

Shredded coconut, to garnish the glass
4 tablespoons (60 ml) white rum
2 tablespoons (30 ml) cream of coconut
1 tablespoon (15 ml) chocolate syrup
Freshly sliced pineapple, to garnish

Place the coconut on a small plate. Dampen the rim of a chilled martini glass with water and dip in the coconut. Shake off the excess. | Fill a cocktail shaker with ice. | Add the rum and cream of coconut. Shake well. | Drizzle the chocolate syrup into a chilled martini glass and strain in the cocktail. | Garnish with the pineapple.

nutty chocolate coffee

Serves 2 | Prep: 5 min | Level: 1

2 oz (60 g) semisweet (dark) chocolate,
   finely chopped
1 cup (250 ml) hot coffee
½ teaspoon almond extract (essence)
1 cup (250 ml) hot milk
Whipped cream, to serve
Chocolate shavings, to serve

Divide the chocolate between two heatproof glasses. | Pour in the hot coffee and stir until the chocolate has partially dissolved. | Add the almond extract and the hot milk. Stir well. | Top with the whipped cream and chocolate shavings.

aztec hot and piquant chocolate

Serves 1 | Prep: 10 min | Level: 1

1 oz (30 g) bittersweet (plain) chocolate,
   coarsely grated
⅔ cup (150 ml) boiling water
1 teaspoon vanilla extract (essence)
Red pepper flakes, to taste

Place the grated chocolate in a medium bowl. Add 1–2 tablespoons of the boiling water and stir to form a paste. | Pour in the remaining water and vanilla. Beat until frothy. | Season with the red pepper flakes to taste. | Serve the chocolate in heatproof glass mugs.

cool irish coffee

Serves 1 | Prep: 10 min | Level: 1

2 tablespoons Irish whiskey
2 tablespoons chocolate cream liqueur
1 tablespoon Kahlùa (coffee liqueur)
1 scoop chocolate ice cream
1 scoop coffee ice cream
Unsweetened cocoa powder,
   to dust

Blend the whiskey, chocolate cream liqueur, Kahlùa, and the ice creams in a food processor or blender until smooth. | Pour the mixture into a mug or glass and dust with the cocoa.

black orchid

Serves 1 | Prep: 5 min | Level: 1

2 tablespoons (30 ml) dark crème de cacao
1 tablespoon (15 ml) blackberry brandy
4 tablespoons (60 ml) cream
Fresh blackberries, to garnish

This is a rich and indulgent cocktail—an ideal to finish off a summer evening.

Fill a cocktail shaker with ice. | Add the crème de cacao, blackberry brandy, and cream. | Shake very briskly to mix and chill. | Pour the cocktail into a chilled martini glass. | Garnish with the blackberries.

death-by-chocolate

Serves 4 | Prep: 5 min | Cooking: 5 min | Level: 1

2 cups (500 ml) heavy (double) cream
2 cups (500 ml) half-and-half
12 oz (300 g) semisweet (dark) chocolate
   chips
2 teaspoons vanilla extract (essence)
Whipped cream, to decorate

Bring the cream and half-and-half to a simmer over medium heat in a large saucepan. | Add the chocolate chips and stir until melted. | Remove from the heat and add the vanilla. Beat until frothy. | Pour into mugs and top with a dollop of whipped cream.

mexican hot chocolate

Serves 3 | Prep: 20 min | Cooking: 20 min | Level: 1

½ cup (125 ml) water
3 oz (90 g) semisweet (dark) chocolate,
   coarsely chopped
1 tablespoon cornstarch (cornflour)
2 cups (500 ml) milk
½ teaspoon ground cinnamon
½ teaspoon vanilla extract (essence)
1 cup (250 ml) whipped cream

The slow simmering and whisking of the hot chocolate renders a sumptuous, bubbling froth.

Bring the water to a boil in a medium saucepan. Lower the heat, add the chocolate, and beat with a whisk until well blended and glossy. | Stir the cornstarch into ½ cup (125 ml) of the milk. | Increase the heat to medium and gradually beat in the cornstarch mixture and the remaining milk. Stir in the cinnamon and vanilla. Bring to a boil, beating often, then remove from the heat. | Let cool for 5 minutes. Return the pan to the heat and simmer over low heat for 5 minutes, stirring often. | The chocolate should be very thick. Use a whisk to beat it until foamy. | Pour the hot chocolate into heatproof glasses or mugs and serve hot with lashings of cream.

dusky hot chocolate cream punch

Serves 8–10 | Prep: 15 min | Level: 1

1¾ cups (450 ml) tequila
1¼ cups (310 ml) Kahlùa (coffee liqueur)
4 tablespoons coffee rum liqueur
1 quart (1 liter) hot chocolate
2 cups (500 ml) light (single) cream
2 oz (60 g) semisweet (dark) chocolate,
  finely grated, to sprinkle

Mix the tequila, Kahlua, coffee rum liqueur, and hot chocolate in a large jug. | Pour the mixture into glasses and top each drink with the cream. It should float on the surface. | Sprinkle with the grated chocolate and serve hot.

banana chocolate milkshake

Serves 2 | Prep: 10 min | Level: 1

1 cup (250 ml) milk
2 tablespoons unsweetened cocoa powder
⅓ cup (70 g) granulated sugar
1 firm-ripe banana, thinly sliced
1 teaspoon vanilla extract (essence)
10–12 ice cubes

Blend the milk, cocoa powder, sugar, banana, and vanilla in a blender until smooth. | Add the ice cubes and pulse until the mixture begins to thicken. | Pour into chilled collins glasses and serve at once.

rich mint chocolate milkshake

Serves 2 | Prep: 25 min | Cooking: 5 min | Level: 1

⅓ cup (50 g) unsweetened cocoa powder
1⅔ cups (400 ml) milk
⅔ cup (150 ml) light (single) cream
½ teaspoon mint extract (essence)
2 scoops chocolate ice cream

Mix the cocoa with 2 tablespoons of milk in a small saucepan to form a smooth paste. | Stir in another 4 tablespoons of milk. Bring to a boil over medium heat, stirring constantly. | Remove from the heat and transfer to a food processor or blender. Pour in the remaining milk, cream, and mint extract and process until frothy. | Pour the mixture into heatproof glasses and drop a scoop of the ice cream into each one. The ice cream should float on the surface.

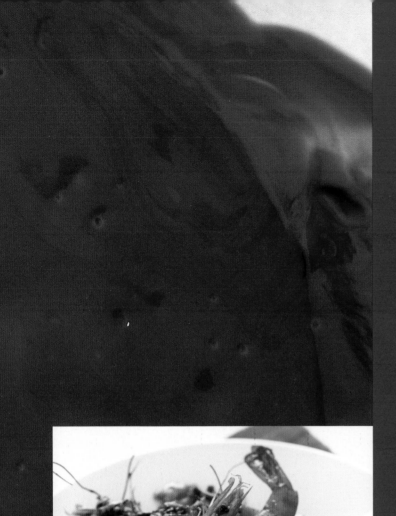

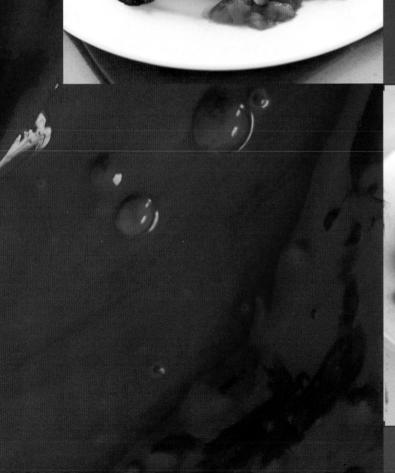

Savory Dishes

"Enjoy this whenever it suits your mood,
Not as a drink but as a much-loved food!"
Johann Wolfgang von Goethe (1749–1832)

shrimp with chocolate sauce

Serves 4 | Prep: 20 min | Cooking: 35 min | Level: 2

½ cup (125 ml) extra-virgin olive oil
2 medium onions, finely chopped
1 bay leaf
1 teaspoon finely chopped thyme
1 small ham bone (optional)
2 lb (1 kg) firm-ripe tomatoes, diced
1 quart (1 liter) water
12 giant shrimp (prawn tails), each weighing
   about 2 oz (60 g), cleaned
Salt and freshly ground black pepper to taste
3 cloves garlic, very finely chopped
½ cup (50 g) toasted, finely chopped almonds
4 oz (125 g) semisweet (dark) chocolate,
   coarsely chopped and melted

Use Dublin Bay prawns, langoustines, or lobsterettes to add authenticity to this flavorsome Catalan dish.

Heat 2 tablespoons of oil in a medium saucepan over medium heat. Sauté the onions, bay leaf, thyme, and ham bone, if using, for 8–10 minutes, or until the onions are lightly browned. | Stir in the tomatoes. Lower the heat and cover and cook for 15 minutes. | Pour in the water and let it reduce by half the volume. Strain the sauce. | Season the shrimp with salt and pepper. | Heat the remaining oil in a large frying pan over medium heat. Fry the shrimp for 8–10 minutes, or until pink. | Remove from the pan, reserving the oil, and arrange on serving plates. Drizzle the strained sauce all over the shrimp. | Mix the garlic, almonds, and chocolate in a small bowl. Pour in 4 tablespoons of the reserved oil and spoon over the shrimp.

mexican turkey mole

Serves 4 | Prep: 45 min | Cooking: 1 hr 30 min | Level: 2

2⅓ lb (1.3 kg) turkey pieces
1 onion, quartered
4 tablespoons blanched almonds
2 tablespoons sesame seeds
2 tablespoons raisins
3 black peppercorns
1 clove
2 teaspoons ground cinnamon
2 teaspoons red chile paste (or more)
¾ cup (180 ml) water
1 onion, finely chopped
2 cloves garlic, finely chopped
3 tomatoes, peeled and chopped
1 cup (60 g) fine dry bread crumbs
1 tablespoon sunflower oil
1 oz (30 g) semisweet (dark) chocolate
Salt and freshly ground black pepper to taste

Poultry, or game, served with chocolate is a match made in heaven. Replace the turkey with chicken, pheasant, or even hare for an equally tasty dish.

Put the turkey pieces into a large saucepan with the onion quarters, cover with water, and simmer for 1 hour until tender. | Strain and reserve the stock. | Skin the meat and cut into bite-sized pieces. | Transfer to a large earthenware pot. | Preheat the oven to 350°F (180°C/gas 4). | Sauté the almonds and sesame seeds in a dry frying pan over medium heat until lightly browned. | Transfer to a food processor and process with the raisins, peppercorns, clove, and cinnamon until finely ground. | Add the chile paste, water, chopped onion, garlic, tomatoes, and bread crumbs and process again until smooth. | Sauté the processed mixture in the oil in a large frying pan over medium heat for about 5 minutes. | Pour ¾ cup (180 ml) of the reserved stock into a small saucepan and add the chocolate. | Stir over low heat until the chocolate has melted. | Add to the sautéed mixture and season with salt and pepper. Pour the sauce over the turkey. | Bake for 20–30 minutes, or until piping hot. | Serve immediately.

chocolate mini muffins with robiola and salami

Makes 20–24 mini muffins | Prep: 40 min + 1 hour
30 min to prove the dough | Cooking: 20 min | Level: 3

For the Mini Muffins
1 oz (30 g) fresh yeast or 2 (¼-oz/7-g)
  packages active dry yeast
¾ cup (180 ml) warm water
7 tablespoons warm milk
3⅓ cups (500 g) all-purpose (plain) flour
4 tablespoons unsweetened cocoa powder
2 teaspoons salt
1 tablespoon sugar
3½ oz (100 g) semisweet (dark) chocolate,
  in shavings
7 tablespoons butter (or lard)
1 teaspoon milk, to brush

For the Topping
1¼ cups (310 g) Robiola cheese
5 oz (150 g) salami (preferably Milano),
  very thinly sliced

This New York deli-style snack is deceptively delicious. Use goat's cheese if Robiola is unavailable.

Mini Muffins: Dissolve the yeast in the water and milk in a large bowl. | Set aside for 10 minutes, or until foamy. | Sift together the flour, cocoa, and salt. | Add the sugar to the yeast mixture. Gradually stir in the sifted dry ingredients. | Transfer to a lightly floured surface and knead for 3 minutes. | Add the chocolate and butter and continue kneading until smooth, evenly colored, and the dough does not stick to your hands. It should be a firm dough. | Shape into a ball and cover with a cloth. Set aside to rise in a warm place for about 1 hour and 30 minutes, or until the dough has doubled in volume. | Preheat the oven to 350°F (180°C/gas 4). | Butter two 12-cup mini muffin pans. | Break the dough into pieces about the size of large walnuts and place them in the prepared cups. | Brush the tops with milk and bake for 15–20 minutes, or until a toothpick inserted into the center comes out clean. | Let cool. | **Topping:** Spoon a dollop of Robiola on the muffins and top with folded slices of salami.

beef tenderloin with chocolate

Serves 4 | Prep: 15 min | Cooking: 30 min | Level: 2

2 lb (1 kg) beef tenderloin, in a single cut
Salt and freshly ground black pepper to taste
3 tablespoons butter
1 small onion, finely chopped
1 clove garlic, finely chopped
1 cup (250 ml) water
½ cup (125 ml) dry white wine
1 oz (30 g) bittersweet (plain) chocolate,
  finely grated
2 tablespoons finely chopped parsley

Season the beef generously with salt and pepper. | Brown the beef in the butter in a large frying pan over high heat until sealed all over. | Add the onion and garlic and sauté over medium heat until the onion has softened. | Pour in the water and wine. Cover and simmer over low heat for 15 minutes. | Add the chocolate and simmer for 10 minutes more. | Slice the beef finely and sprinkle with the parsley.

venison in chocolate sauce

Serves 4 | Prep: 30 min + overnight to marinate the venison | Cooking: 1 hr 40 min | Level: 2

2 lb (1 kg) venison steak, cut in bite-sized dice

For the Marinade
¾ cup (180 ml) dry red wine
10 juniper berries
1 bay leaf
1 shallot and carrot, coarsely chopped
½ stalk celery, coarsely chopped
½ stick cinnamon
1 clove

5 tablespoons extra-virgin olive oil
1 red onion, finely chopped
1 carrot, finely chopped
1 stalk celery, finely chopped
2 cloves garlic, finely chopped
2 tablespoons finely chopped parsley
2 tablespoons tomato concentrate mixed in
   2 cups (500 ml) homemade beef stock
2 tablespoons each diced mixed candied fruit,
   pine nuts, and golden raisins (sultanas)
2 oz (60 g) semisweet (dark) chocolate,
   in shavings
4 tablespoons each white vinegar and sugar

Place the venison in a large glass bowl with the ingredients for the marinade and leave overnight. | Remove the venison from the marinade. Filter the liquid and set aside. | Place the oil in a large saucepan and sauté the finely chopped red onion, carrot, and celery over medium heat for 5 minutes. | Add the venison, garlic, and parsley and sauté for 3 minutes more. | Gradually pour in the filtered marinade and cook over high heat until the wine has evaporated. | Pour in the stock with the tomato concentrate. Cover and cook over low heat for about 1 hour and 30 minutes, or until the venison is very tender. | Mix together the candied fruit, pine nuts, raisins, chocolate, vinegar, and sugar and add to the stew. Stir until the chocolate has melted. | Serve hot with boiled potatoes.

chocolate fettuccine with butter, sage, and mozzarella

Serves 4 | Prep: 50 min + 30 min to rest the pasta | Cooking: 10 min | Level: 2

For the Pasta
2⅓ cups (350 g) all-purpose (plain) flour
⅓ cup (50 g) unsweetened cocoa powder
Pinch of salt
3 large eggs, lightly beaten
Semolina flour, to sprinkle

For the Sauce
⅔ cup (150 g) butter
24 fresh sage leaves
12 bocconcini of Mozzarella (about the size
   of a quail's egg), well drained
Freshly ground pink pepper or red pepper
   flakes to taste

Pasta: Sift the flour, cocoa powder, and salt onto a clean surface (preferably made of wood) and make a well in the center. | Pour the beaten eggs into the well. Use your fingertips to gradually incorporate the eggs into the flour. Take care not to break the wall of flour or the eggs will run. | Gather the dough up into a ball. Knead the dough for 20 minutes, until smooth and silky. | Wrap the dough in plastic wrap (cling film) and let rest for 30 minutes. | Divide the dough into pieces. Roll a piece of dough through the machine at the thickest setting. Continue rolling the dough through the machine, reducing the thickness setting one notch at a time down to the required thickness. You may need to fold the pasta as you work to obtain an evenly shaped sheet. Sprinkle with semolina and cover with a clean dry cloth. Set the machine to cut to ¼-inch (5-mm) wide and run each sheet through. | Cook the pasta in a large pot of salted, boiling water until al dente. | **Sauce:** While the pasta is cooking, melt the butter and sage in a small saucepan. | Drain the pasta and toss gently with the butter and sage. Take a large pasta fork and wrap about a quarter of the pasta around it to make a nest. Place 3 Mozzarellas in the center and season with freshly ground pink pepper. Repeat with the remaining pasta and Mozzarella.

gnocchi with golden raisins and cocoa

Serves 6 | Prep: 1 hr | Cooking: 40 min | Level: 2

For the Gnocchi
3 lb (1.5 kg) mealy (floury) potatoes
2 large eggs
2 tablespoons freshly grated Parmesan cheese
Salt and freshly ground white pepper to taste
3⅓ cups (500 g) all-purpose (plain) flour

For the Sauce
1 tablespoon unsweetened cocoa powder
2 tablespoons golden raisins (sultanas),
    soaked in warm water and drained
½ cup (60 g) freshly grated Parmesan cheese
½ cup (60 g) freshly grated Ricotta Salata
    cheese, preferably smoked
½ cup (125 g) butter, melted
⅓ cup (30 g) finely chopped candied
    lemon peel
Pinch of ground cinnamon
Salt and freshly ground white pepper to taste

Gnocchi: Cook the potatoes in salted, boiling water for 15–20 minutes, or until tender. | Drain and peel them. Press the potatoes through a potato ricer onto a clean surface. | Work in the eggs and Parmesan and season with salt and pepper. Add enough flour to form a stiff, malleable dough. Break off pieces of dough and form into logs. Cut into 1-inch (2.5-cm) lengths. Dust with the remaining flour. Do not leave the gnocchi too long before cooking because they will stick. | Cook the gnocchi in small batches in a large pot of salted, boiling water until they bob to the surface. | **Sauce:** Mix the cocoa, raisins, Parmesan, Ricotta Salata, half the butter, candied lemon peel, cinnamon, and salt and pepper in a large bowl. | Use a slotted spoon to transfer the gnocchi to the bowl and toss them gently until well coated. Drizzle with the remaining melted butter and sprinkle with the Parmesan. | Serve hot.

venetian ravioli

Serves 4 | Prep: 2 hr + 30 min to rest the dough | Cooking: 15 min | Level: 3

For the Pasta
2⅔ cups (400 g) all purpose (plain) flour
Pinch of salt
2 large eggs
2 tablespoons butter, melted
1 tablespoon water + more if needed

For the Filling
½ medium onion, finely chopped
1 tablespoon butter
1 cup (250 g) cooked spinach, finely chopped
2 tablespoons grated semisweet chocolate
¼ cup (45 g) raisins
¼ cup (30 g) day-old rye bread crumbs
2 tablespoons chopped candied citron peel
1 large egg
1 tablespoon finely chopped fresh parsley
1 teaspoon sugar
Pinch of ground cinnamon
Salt and freshly ground black pepper to taste
6 tablespoons butter, melted
¾ cup (90 g) grated Ricotta Salata cheese
Pinch of sugar

Pasta: Sift the flour and salt onto a clean surface and make a well in the center. Break the eggs into the well and mix in with the butter and enough water to make a smooth dough. Knead for 15–20 minutes, until smooth and elastic. Gather the dough up into a ball, wrap in plastic wrap (cling film), and let rest for 30 minutes. | **Filling:** Sauté the onion in the butter in a large frying pan over medium heat for 5 minutes until softened. | Add the spinach and sauté for 1 minute. | Remove from the heat and transfer to a large bowl. | Mix in the chocolate, raisins, bread crumbs, citron peel, egg, parsley, sugar, and cinnamon. Season with salt and pepper. The mixture should hold its shape, if it seems too fluid, add more bread crumbs. | Roll the dough out on a lightly floured surface until paper-thin. Cut out 3-inch (8-cm) rounds. | Drop two teaspoons of filling into the centers of the rounds. Fold in half and seal well. | Cook the pasta in small batches in a large pot of salted, boiling water for 3–4 minutes, until al dente. | Use a slotted spoon to transfer the ravioli to a serving bowl and arrange in layers with the melted butter, Ricotta Salata, and sugar.

Cookies and Muffins

"There's nothing better than a good friend,
except a good friend with chocolate."
Charles Dickens, The Pickwick Papers (1812–1870)

classic hazelnut and honey florentines

Makes 22–25 cookies | Prep: 40 min + 30 min to set |
Cooking: 10 min | Level: 1

1 lb (500 g) hazelnuts
1 cup (200 g) granulated sugar
1 cup (250 g) butter, softened
½ cup (125 ml) honey
½ cup (125 ml) heavy (double) cream
Pinch of salt
6 oz (180 g) white chocolate,
   coarsely chopped

Preheat the oven to 325°F/170°C/gas 3. | Spread the hazelnuts on a large baking sheet. Toast for 7 minutes, or until lightly golden. | Transfer to a large cotton kitchen towel. Fold the towel over the nuts and rub them to remove the thin inner skins. Pick out the nuts. | Transfer to a food processor with ¼ cup (50 g) of the sugar and process until very finely chopped. | Increase the oven temperature to 375°F/190°C/gas 5. | Line three cookie sheets with parchment paper. Butter the paper. | Melt the butter with the honey, cream, and the remaining sugar in a small saucepan over low heat until the sugar has dissolved completely. | Bring to a boil and boil for 2 minutes. | Remove from the heat and stir in the hazelnut mixture and salt. | Drop teaspoons of the mixture 3 inches (8 cm) apart onto the prepared cookie sheets. | Bake, one sheet at a time, for 8–10 minutes, or until golden brown. | Cool on the sheets until the cookies firm slightly. | Transfer to racks to cool. | Melt the chocolate in a double boiler over barely simmering water. Spread over the bottom of the cookies and use a fork to create a wave pattern. Let stand on waxed paper for 30 minutes until set.

hazelnut and mocha biscotti

Makes about 24 cookies | Prep: 35 min + 30 min to set |
Cooking: 45 min | Level: 2

¾ cup (125 g) hazelnuts
1⅓ cups (200 g) all-purpose (plain) flour
½ cup (75 g) unsweetened cocoa powder
1½ teaspoons baking soda
   (bicarbonate of soda)
Pinch of salt
3 large eggs
1 cup (200 g) granulated sugar
½ teaspoon vanilla extract (essence)
2 teaspoons freeze-dried coffee granules
⅓ cup (60 g) semisweet (dark) chocolate chips
8 oz (250 g) white chocolate,
   coarsely chopped

Preheat the oven to 325°F (170°C/gas 3). | Spread the hazelnuts on a large baking sheet. Toast for 7 minutes, or until lightly golden. Transfer to a large cotton kitchen towel. Fold the towel over the nuts and rub them to remove the thin inner skins. Pick out the nuts. | Increase the oven temperature to 350°F (180°C/gas 4). | Butter a cookie sheet. | Sift the flour, cocoa, baking soda, and salt into a medium bowl. | Beat the eggs, sugar, and vanilla in a large bowl with an electric mixer at high speed until pale and thick. | Mix in the dry ingredients, coffee granules, chocolate chips, and hazelnuts to form a stiff dough. | Divide the dough in half. Form into two 12-inch (30-cm) logs and place 2 inches (5-cm) apart on the prepared cookie sheet, flattening them slightly. | Bake for 25–30 minutes, or until firm to the touch. | Transfer to a cutting board to cool for 15 minutes. | Lower the oven temperature to 325°F (170°C/gas 3). | Cut on the diagonal into 1-inch (2.5-cm) slices. | Arrange the slices cut-side down on two cookie sheets and bake for 10–15 minutes, or until golden and toasted. | Transfer to racks to cool. | Melt the white chocolate in a double boiler over barely simmering water. Drizzle the chocolate over the biscotti and let stand on waxed paper for 30 minutes until set.

banana kipferl

Makes 45–50 cookies | Prep: 40 min + 60 min to chill and stand | Cooking: 12 min | Level: 2

1²⁄₃ cups (250 g) all-purpose (plain) flour
1 teaspoon baking powder
Pinch of salt
²⁄₃ cup (150 g) butter, softened
½ cup (100 g) granulated sugar
1 large egg yolk
1 vanilla pod
1 cup (100 g) broken-up, dried, unsweetened
   banana chips
3½ oz (100 g) semisweet (dark) chocolate,
   coarsely chopped
3½ oz (100 g) white chocolate,
   coarsely chopped

Sift the flour, baking powder, and salt into a medium bowl. | Beat the butter and sugar in a large bowl with an electric mixer at high speed until creamy. | Add the egg yolk, beating until just blended. | Scoop out the pulp from the vanilla pod and add to the mixture. | Mix in the dry ingredients and banana chips to form a smooth dough. | Divide the dough in half. | Form into 10-inch (25-cm) logs, wrap in plastic wrap (cling film), and refrigerate for 30 minutes. | Preheat the oven to 350°F (180°C/gas 4). | Line three cookie sheets with parchment paper. | Discard the plastic wrap. Slice the dough ½-inch (1-cm) thick. | Press the centers inward and taper the ends to form crescents. | Place 1 inch (2.5 cm) apart on the prepared cookie sheets. | Bake, one sheet at a time, for 10–12 minutes, or until just golden at the edges. | Transfer on the parchment paper to a rack and let cool completely. | Melt the chocolates separately in double boilers over barely simmering water. | Dip one cookie end into the white chocolate and the other end into the semisweet chocolate. | Let stand on waxed paper for 30 minutes.

rose leaf chocolate cookies

Makes 30–32 cookies | Prep: 40 min + 30 min to chill | Cooking: 12 min | Level: 2

For the Rose Leaf Decorations
6 oz (180 g) bittersweet (plain) chocolate,
   coarsely chopped
30–32 green rose leaves, washed and dried

For the Cookies
1½ cups (225 g) all-purpose (plain) flour
1 tablespoon unsweetened cocoa powder
1 teaspoon baking powder
Pinch of salt
½ cup (125 g) butter, softened
¾ cup (150 g) granulated sugar
1 large egg

Rose Leaf Decorations: Melt the chocolate in a double boiler over barely simmering water. Use a small pastry brush to paint the melted chocolate onto the underside of each rose leaf. | Keep any remaining chocolate in the double boiler. Leave the decorations to set at room temperature for at least 30 minutes—do not refrigerate. When the chocolate has set, carefully peel off the rose leaves. | **Cookies:** Preheat the oven to 400°F (200°C/gas 6). | Line two cookie sheets with parchment paper. | Sift the flour, cocoa, baking powder, and salt into a medium bowl. | Beat the butter and sugar in a large bowl with an electric mixer at high speed until creamy. | Add the egg, beating until just blended. | Mix in the dry ingredients to form a stiff dough. | Form the dough into two logs 1½ inches (4 cm) in diameter. Wrap in plastic wrap (cling film) and refrigerate for 30 minutes. | Discard the plastic wrap. Slice the dough ¼ inch (5 mm) thick. | Transfer the cookies to the prepared cookie sheets, placing them 3 inches (8 cm) apart. | Bake for 8–10 minutes, or until golden, rotating the sheets halfway through for even browning. | Transfer to racks to cool. | Heat the remaining chocolate in the double boiler over barely simmering water until liquid. Brush a little chocolate onto each cookie and lay a rose leaf decoration on top.

orange, choc chip, and walnut cookies

Makes about 30 cookies | Prep: 15 min | Cooking: 12 min | Level: 1

2 cups (300 g) all-purpose (plain) flour
½ cup (75 g) whole-wheat (wholemeal) flour
1 teaspoon baking soda (bicarbonate of soda)
½ teaspoon salt
¾ cup (180 g) butter
1 cup (200 g) granulated sugar
½ cup (100 g) firmly packed brown sugar
2 tablespoons finely grated orange zest
2 large eggs
1 cup (100 g) finely chopped walnuts
6 oz (180 g) semisweet (dark) chocolate chips

Be sure to use a dark brown sugar in these cookies, or add 1 tablespoon of molasses. The orange and chocolate need the deep, dark flavor of unprocessed sugar to show themselves to the full.

Preheat the oven to 350°F (180°C/gas 4). | Butter two cookie sheets and line with waxed paper. | Sift both flours, baking soda, and salt into a large bowl. | Beat the butter, both sugars, and the orange zest in a large bowl with an electric mixer at high speed until pale and creamy. | Add the eggs, one at a time, beating until just blended after each addition. | With mixer at low speed, gradually beat in the dry ingredients, followed by the walnuts and the chocolate chips. | Drop tablespoons of the batter 1 inch (2.5 cm) apart on the prepared cookie sheets. | Bake for 10–12 minutes, or until golden and lightly cracked on top. | Cool on the sheets for 5 minutes. Transfer to racks to cool completely.

double chocolate drops

Makes about 36 cookies | Prep: 25 min | Cooking: 10 min | Level: 1

1⅓ cups (200 g) all-purpose (plain) flour
½ teaspoon baking soda
   (bicarbonate of soda)
Pinch of salt
2 oz (60 g) semisweet (dark) chocolate,
   coarsely chopped
½ cup (125 g) butter, softened
1 cup (200 g) granulated sugar
1 teaspoon vanilla extract (essence)
1 large egg, lightly beaten
2 tablespoons milk

For the Chocolate Frosting
2 oz (60 g) semisweet (dark) chocolate,
   coarsely chopped
4 tablespoons butter, softened
1⅓ cups (200 g) confectioners' (icing) sugar
½ cup (50 g) pecans, halved

Preheat the oven to 400°F (200°C/gas 6). | Butter three cookie sheets. | Sift the flour, baking soda, and salt into a large bowl. | Melt the chocolate in a double boiler over barely simmering water. | Beat the butter, sugar, and melted chocolate in a large bowl with an electric mixer at high speed until creamy. | Add the vanilla and egg, beating until just blended. | Mix in the dry ingredients and milk until well blended. | Drop teaspoons of the dough 1 inch (2.5 cm) apart onto the prepared cookie sheets. | Bake, one sheet at a time, for 8–10 minutes, or until slightly risen. | Cool on the sheets until the cookies firm slightly. | Transfer to racks to finish cooling. | **Chocolate Frosting:** Melt the chocolate in a double boiler over barely simmering water. | With mixer at high speed, beat the butter and melted chocolate in a medium bowl until creamy. | Beat in the confectioners' sugar until well blended. | Spread the frosting over the tops of the cookies and decorate with the pecans.

black pepper
chocolate chip cookies

Makes about 18 cookies | Prep: 15 minutes | Cooking: 12 min | Level: 1

½ cup (75 g) all-purpose (plain) flour
½ teaspoon baking powder
½ teaspoon freshly ground black pepper
Pinch of salt
½ cup (60 g) raisins
2 tablespoons coffee liqueur
8 oz (250 g) bittersweet (plain) chocolate, coarsely chopped
4 tablespoons butter
2 large eggs
¾ cup (150 g) granulated sugar
2 teaspoons vanilla extract (essence)
1 cup (180 g) semisweet (dark) chocolate chips

Preheat the oven to 350°F (180°C/gas 4). | Butter a cookie sheet and line with waxed paper. | Sift the flour, baking powder, pepper, and salt into a small bowl. | Heat the raisins and coffee liqueur in a small saucepan over low heat. | Melt the chocolate with the butter in a double boiler over barely simmering water. Set aside to cool. | Beat the eggs and sugar in a large bowl with an electric mixer at high speed until very pale and creamy, about 5 minutes. | With mixer at medium speed, beat in the chocolate and vanilla. | With mixer at low speed, beat in the dry ingredients, followed by the raisin mixture and the chocolate chips. | Drop tablespoons of the dough 1 inch (2.5 cm) apart on the prepared cookie sheet. | Bake for 10–12 minutes, or until risen slightly. | Cool on the sheets until the cookies firm slightly. | Transfer to racks to finish cooling.

banana
chocolate chip muffins

Makes 20 muffins | Prep: 20 min | Cooking: 30 min | Level: 1

1 cup (150 g) whole-wheat (wholemeal) flour
1 cup (150 g) all-purpose (plain) flour
2 teaspoons baking powder
½ teaspoon baking soda (bicarbonate of soda)
Pinch of salt
½ cup (125 g) unsalted butter, softened
1 cup (200 g) granulated sugar
3 large eggs
2 large very ripe bananas, mashed
4 tablespoons milk
1 cup (180 g) semisweet (dark) chocolate chips
1 cup (100 g) chopped walnuts

Preheat the oven to 375°F (190°C/gas 5). | Arrange 20 foil or paper baking cups on baking sheets. | Sift both flours, baking powder, baking soda, and salt into a large bowl. | Beat the butter and sugar in a large bowl with an electric mixer at medium speed until creamy. | Add the eggs, one at a time, beating until just blended after each addition. | With mixer at low speed, beat in the bananas, followed by the dry ingredients, alternating with the milk. | Stir in the chocolate chips and walnuts. | Spoon the batter into the cups, filling each three-quarters full. | Bake for 20–30 minutes, or until a toothpick inserted into the center comes out clean. | Cool the muffins on racks.

chocolate muffins

Makes about 16 muffins | Prep: 15 min | Cooking: 25 min | Level: 1

2 cups (300 g) all-purpose (plain) flour
½ cup (75 g) unsweetened cocoa powder
2 teaspoons baking powder
Pinch of salt
½ cup (125 g) butter, softened
1¼ cups (250 g) granulated sugar
1 tablespoon honey
2 large eggs
¾ cup (180 ml) milk
⅓ cup (60 g) semisweet (dark)
   chocolate chips

Preheat the oven to 350°F (180°C/gas 4). | Butter 16 muffin-pan cups or line with foil or paper baking cups. | Sift the flour, cocoa, baking powder, and salt into a large bowl. | Beat the butter, sugar, and honey in a large bowl with an electric mixer at medium speed until creamy. | Add the eggs, one at a time, beating until just blended after each addition. | With mixer at low speed, gradually beat in the dry ingredients, alternating with the milk. Stir in the chocolate chips. | Spoon the batter into the prepared cups. | Bake for 20–25 minutes, or until a toothpick inserted into the centers comes out clean. | Cool the muffins on racks.

chocolate and cherry muffins

Makes about 12 muffins | Prep: 15 min | Cooking: 20 min | Level: 1

1½ cups (225 g) all-purpose (plain) flour
⅓ cup (50 g) unsweetened cocoa powder
2 teaspoons baking powder
Pinch of salt
2 large eggs
½ cup (100 g) firmly packed brown sugar
½ cup (125 g) butter, melted
¾ cup (180 ml) milk
24 red candied cherries, halved

Preheat the oven to 375°F (190°C/gas 5). | Butter and flour a 12-cup muffin pan or line with foil or paper baking cups. | Sift the flour, cocoa, baking powder, and salt into a large bowl. | Beat the eggs, brown sugar, and butter in a medium bowl with an electric mixer at high speed until creamy. | Mix in the milk. | Stir into the dry ingredients. | Spoon the batter into the prepared cups, filling each three-quarters full. Press four pieces of candied cherry into each muffin, leaving 1 or 2 pieces visible on top. | Bake for 15–20 minutes, or until springy to the touch. | Cool the muffins on racks.

easter chocolate muffins

Makes about 12 muffins | Prep: 10 min | Cooking: 20 min | Level: 1

1½ cups (225 g) all-purpose (plain) flour
½ cup (100 g) granulated sugar
½ cup (75 g) unsweetened cocoa powder
2 large eggs, lightly beaten
6 tablespoons butter, melted
2 teaspoons vanilla extract (essence)
2 teaspoons baking powder
20 small solid chocolate Easter eggs
2 tablespoons chocolate chips (optional)

Children will love these muffins at Eastertime. Throughout the rest of the year, replace the Easter egg with a small square of semisweet chocolate.

Preheat the oven to 350°F (180°C/gas 4). | Butter and flour a 12-cup muffin pan or line with foil or paper baking cups. | Beat the flour, sugar, cocoa, eggs, butter, vanilla, and baking powder in a large bowl with an electric mixer at medium speed until well blended. | Spoon half the batter into the cups. Place a chocolate egg in each. Top each with the remaining batter. | Sprinkle each with a few chocolate chips, if using. | Bake for 15–20 minutes, or until springy to the touch. | Cool the muffins on racks.

frosted chocolate muffins

Makes 20 muffins | Prep: 20 min | Cooking: 25 min | Level: 1

4 oz (125 g) semisweet (dark) chocolate, coarsely chopped
1 tablespoon heavy (double) cream
2 cups (300 g) all-purpose (plain) flour
2 teaspoons baking powder
Pinch of salt
¾ cup (180 g) butter, softened
1½ cups (300 g) granulated sugar
3 large eggs
⅔ cup (150 ml) milk
2 teaspoons vanilla extract (essence)

For the Chocolate Frosting
2 cups (300 g) confectioners' (icing) sugar
2 tablespoons unsweetened cocoa powder
2 tablespoons butter, softened
1 teaspoon vanilla extract (essence)
About 2 tablespoons boiling water

Preheat the oven to 350°F (180°C/gas 4). | Line 20 muffin-pan cups with foil or paper baking cups. | Melt the chocolate with the cream in a double boiler over barely simmering water. Set aside to cool. | Sift the flour, baking powder, and salt into a large bowl. | Beat the butter and sugar in a large bowl with an electric mixer at medium speed until creamy. | Add the eggs, one at a time, beating until just blended after each addition. | With mixer at low speed, gradually beat in the melted chocolate mixture, followed by the dry ingredients, alternating with the milk and vanilla. | Spoon the batter into the prepared pans, filling each two-thirds full. | Bake for 20–25 minutes, or until a toothpick inserted into the center comes out clean. | Cool the muffins on racks. | **Chocolate Frosting:** Stir together the confectioners' sugar and cocoa in a double boiler. Add the butter, vanilla, and enough of the water to make a firm paste. Stir over simmering water until the frosting has a spreadable consistency. | Spread the frosting over the tops of the muffins.

strawberry and white chocolate muffins

Makes about 12 muffins | Prep: 15 min | Cooking: 30 min | Level: 1

1½ cups (225 g) all-purpose (plain) flour
2 teaspoons baking powder
Pinch of salt
½ cup (100 g) granulated sugar
½ cup (125 g) butter, melted
½ cup (125 ml) milk
1 large egg
½ teaspoon vanilla extract (essence)
1½ cups (270 g) white chocolate chips
½ cup (160 ml) strawberry preserves or jam

Preheat the oven to 350°F (180°C/gas 4). | Line a 12-cup muffin pan with foil or paper baking cups. | Sift the flour, baking powder, and salt into a large bowl. Stir in the sugar. | Beat the butter, milk, egg, and vanilla in a medium bowl until well blended. Stir the milk mixture into the dry ingredients, followed by the chocolate chips. | Spoon three-quarters of the batter into the prepared cups. Spoon a heaping 1 teaspoon strawberry preserves into each muffin, making a hole in the batter. Top with the remaining batter. | Bake for 25–30 minutes, or until a toothpick inserted into the center comes out clean. | Cool the muffins on racks.

honey and white chocolate muffins

Makes about 18 muffins | Prep: 10 min | Cooking: 20 min | Level: 1

2 cups (300 g) all-purpose (plain) flour
2½ teaspoons baking powder
Pinch of salt
¼ cup (50 g) granulated sugar
1½ cups (270 g) white chocolate chips
1 cup (250 ml) milk
4 tablespoons butter, melted
1 large egg, lightly beaten
2 tablespoons honey
2 teaspoons vanilla extract (essence)

Preheat the oven to 400°F (200°C/gas 6). | Arrange 20 foil baking cups on baking sheets. | Sift the flour, baking powder, and salt into a large bowl. Stir in the sugar and chocolate chips. Make a well in the center. | Stir in the milk, butter, egg, honey, and vanilla. | Spoon the batter into the cups, filling each three-quarters full. | Bake for 15–20 minutes, or until a toothpick inserted into the center comes out clean. | Cool the muffins on racks.

coffee and hazelnut macaroons

Makes about 60 cookies | Prep: 25 min | Cooking: 20 min | Level: 2

3 large egg whites
Pinch of salt
1 cup (200 g) superfine (caster) sugar
2 cups (300 g) finely ground hazelnuts
2 teaspoons freeze-dried coffee granules
1 tablespoon Dutch-process cocoa powder
3 oz (90 g) white chocolate, coarsely chopped
60 coffee beans, to decorate

Preheat the oven to 300°F (150°C/gas 2). | Line four cookie sheets with parchment paper. | Beat the egg whites and salt in a large bowl with an electric mixer at medium speed until frothy. | With mixer at high speed, gradually add the superfine sugar, beating until stiff, glossy peaks form. | Use a large rubber spatula to fold in the hazelnuts, coffee granules, and cocoa. | Fit a pastry bag with a plain ½-inch (1-cm) tip. Fill the pastry bag, twist the opening tightly closed, and squeeze out mounds the size of walnuts, spacing them 1 inch (2.5 cm) apart on the prepared cookie sheets. | Bake, one sheet at a time, for 15–20 minutes, or until crisp and dry. | Transfer to racks on the parchment paper to cool. | Melt the chocolate in a double boiler over barely simmering water. | Drizzle the chocolate over the meringues and decorate with coffee beans.

sacher torte cookies

Makes 40–45 cookies | Prep: 25 min + 30 min to stand | Cooking: 15 min | Level: 1

2 cups (300 g) all-purpose (plain) flour
2 tablespoons Dutch-process cocoa powder
Pinch of salt
1 cup (250 g) butter, softened
¼ cup (50 g) granulated sugar
1 large egg
½ cup (160 g) apricot preserves or jam

For the Rich Chocolate Glaze
7 oz (200 g) semisweet (dark) chocolate, coarsely chopped
2 tablespoons butter

These cookies take their flavor from the rich Viennese chocolate cake that was first invented in 1832 by a 16-year-old apprentice chef, Franz Sacher.

Preheat the oven to 350°F (180°C/gas 4). | Butter three cookie sheets. | Sift the flour, cocoa, and salt into a medium bowl. | Beat the butter and sugar in a large bowl with an electric mixer at high speed until creamy. | Add the egg, beating until just blended. | Mix in the dry ingredients to form a smooth dough. | Form the dough into balls the size of walnuts and place 2 inches (5 cm) apart on the prepared cookie sheets. Press your thumb into each one to make a small hollow. | Bake, one batch at a time, for 12–15 minutes, or until firm to the touch. | Transfer to racks to cool. | Fill the hollows with a small amount of preserves. | **Rich Chocolate Glaze:** Melt the chocolate and butter in a double boiler over barely simmering water. | Spoon the glaze into a small freezer bag and cut off a tiny corner. | Pipe over the cookies in a decorative manner and let stand for 30 minutes until set.

Tarts and Pies

"Chocolate is a perfect food, as wholesome as it is delicious,
a beneficent restorer of exhausted power.
It is the best friend of those engaged in literary pursuits."
Baron Justus von Liebig (1803–1873)

chocolate tart with berries

Serves 6–8 | Prep: 30 min + 4 hr to chill | Level: 1

1½ cups (180 g) finely crushed vanilla wafers
⅔ cup (100 g) finely ground almonds
¾ cup (180 g) butter, melted
2 cups (500 ml) Chocolate Pastry Cream
  (see recipe Almond Chocolate Tart, below)
1¼ cups (310 g) mixed berries
4 tablespoons apricot preserves or jam

Mix the vanilla crumbs, almonds, and butter in a large bowl. | Firmly press into the bottom and up the sides of a 9-inch (23-cm) springform pan. | Refrigerate for 2 hours, or until set. | Spoon the pastry cream into the crumb base, taking care not to disturb the crumbs. Refrigerate for 2 hours. | Decorate with the berries. | Heat the apricot preserves in a small pan until liquid and brush over the berries. | Loosen and remove the pan sides to serve.

almond chocolate tart

Serves 6–8 | Prep: 30 min + 1 hr to chill | Cooking: 30 min | Level: 2

For the Chocolate Pastry
4 oz (125 g) bittersweet (plain) chocolate,
  coarsely chopped
1⅓ cups (200 g) all-purpose (plain) flour
½ teaspoon salt
1⅓ cups (200 g) finely ground almonds
¾ cup (180 g) butter, softened
½ cup (100 g) granulated sugar
3 large egg yolks, at room temperature

For the Chocolate Pastry Cream
5 large egg yolks
⅔ cup (140 g) granulated sugar
2 cups (500 ml) milk
⅓ cup (50 g) all-purpose (plain) flour
⅛ teaspoon vanilla extract (essence)
Pinch of salt
7 oz (200 g) bittersweet (plain) chocolate,
  coarsely chopped
1 cup (250 ml) heavy (double) cream

Chocolate Pastry: Melt the chocolate in a double boiler over barely simmering water. Set aside to cool until warm. | Sift the flour and salt into a large bowl. Stir in the almonds. | Beat the butter and sugar in a large bowl with an electric mixer at high speed until creamy. | Add the egg yolks, one at a time, beating until just blended after each addition. | With mixer at low speed, beat in the dry ingredients, followed by the melted chocolate. | Press the dough into a disk, wrap in plastic wrap (cling film), and refrigerate for 30 minutes. | Preheat the oven to 350°F (180°C/ gas 4). | Roll the pastry out on a lightly floured surface into a 10-inch (25-cm) round. Press the dough into a 9-inch (23-cm) springform pan, trimming the edges to fit. Prick all over with a fork. | Bake for 25–30 minutes, or until firm to the touch. | Cool completely in the pan. | **Chocolate Pastry Cream:** Beat the egg yolks and sugar in a double boiler over barely simmering water until pale and thick. | Bring the milk to a boil in a medium saucepan. Add the flour, vanilla, and salt. | Gradually pour the milk into the egg mixture. Cook over low heat, stirring constantly with a wooden spoon, until the mixture registers 160°F (71°C) on an instant-read thermometer. | Melt the chocolate in a double boiler over barely simmering water. | Stir the chocolate into the pastry cream. Let cool completely. | Fill the tart with the pastry cream. | Beat the cream in a medium bowl until stiff. | Spread the cream over the tart. Loosen and remove the pan sides to serve.

creamy chocolate crostata

Serves 6–8 | Prep: 30 min + 30 min to chill | Cooking: 1 hr | Level: 2

For the Shortcrust Pastry

2 cups (300 g) all-purpose (plain) flour
1½ teaspoons salt
4 tablespoons butter
5-6 tablespoons cold water
2-3 tablespoons vanilla wafer crumbs

For the Creamy Chocolate Filling

½ cup (125 g) butter, softened
1 cup (200 g) granulated sugar
6 oz (180 g) bittersweet (plain) chocolate, coarsely chopped
2 tablespoons cornstarch (cornflour)
1 teaspoon vanilla extract (essence)
4 tablespoons milk
4 large eggs, separated
1 cup (250 ml) heavy (double) cream
2 tablespoons unsweetened cocoa powder, to dust

Shortcrust Pastry: Sift the flour and salt into a large bowl. | Use your fingertips to rub in the butter until the mixture resembles coarse crumbs. Mix in enough water to bind the dough. | Press the dough into a disk, wrap in plastic wrap (cling film), and refrigerate for 30 minutes. | Preheat the oven to 375°F (190°C/gas 5). | Set out a 9-inch (23-cm) springform pan. Sprinkle with the crumbs. | Roll the dough out on a lightly floured surface to a 9-inch (23-cm) round. Fit into the pan. | **Creamy Chocolate Filling:** Melt the butter in a saucepan over low heat. | Stir in the sugar, chocolate, cornstarch, and vanilla. | Add the milk and egg yolks and cook, stirring often, for about 10 minutes, or until the filling thickens. Remove from the heat and set aside to cool. | Beat the egg whites in a large bowl with an electric mixer at medium speed until stiff peaks form. | Use a large rubber spatula to fold the beaten whites into the chocolate filling. | Spoon into the pastry shell. | Bake for 50-60 minutes, or until set. | Cool completely in the pan on a rack. | Loosen and remove the pan sides. Dust with the cocoa just before serving.

chocolate meringue pie

Serves 6–8 | Prep: 45 min | Cooking: 70 min | Level: 2

1 lb (500 g) Shortcrust Pastry
  (see Creamy chocolate crostata, above)
1¼ cups (310 ml) sweetened condensed milk
1 teaspoon vanilla extract (essence)
2 cups (400 g) granulated sugar
⅓ cup (50 g) unsweetened cocoa powder
2 tablespoons all-purpose (plain) flour
4 large eggs, separated
4 tablespoons butter, cut up

Preheat the oven to 375°F (190°C/gas 5). | Set out a 9-inch (23-cm) springform pan. | Roll the pastry out on a lightly floured surface to a 9-inch (23-cm) round. Fit into the pan. | Bake for 15-20 minutes, or until lightly browned. | Cool completely in the pan. | Mix the condensed milk and vanilla in a medium saucepan over low heat, stirring constantly, for 3 minutes. | Stir in ¾ cup (150 g) of the sugar, cocoa, and flour until well blended. | Add the egg yolks, beating until just blended. | Mix in the butter and cook until the butter has melted. | Spoon the mixture into the pastry case. | Lower the oven temperature to 350°F (180°C/gas 4). | Bake for 35-40 minutes, or until set and firm to the touch. | Beat the egg whites in a large bowl with an electric mixer at medium speed until soft peaks form. With mixer at high speed, gradually add the remaining sugar, beating until stiff, glossy peaks form. | Spread the meringue over the cooled filling. | Bake for 8-10 minutes, or until the meringue is golden. | Serve warm.

divine mousse pie

Serves 6–8 | Prep: 45 min + 1 hr 30 min to chill |
Cooking: 20 min | Level: 2

1 lb (500 g) Shortcrust Pastry
  (see Creamy chocolate crostata, left)
1 recipe Chocolate Mousse (see page 130)
1 cup (250 ml) heavy (double) cream
2 tablespoons unsweetened cocoa powder
2 tablespoons confectioners' (icing) sugar
1 teaspoon amaretto or other almond liqueur

Add the flavoring of your choice to the cream topping. Substitute rum or a mint liqueur for the almond liqueur.

Preheat the oven to 375°F (190°C/gas 5). | Set out a 9-inch (23-cm) springform pan. | Roll the pastry out on a lightly floured surface to a 9-inch (23-cm) round. Fit into the pan. | Bake for 15–20 minutes, or until lightly browned. | Cool completely in the pan. | Spoon the mousse into the prepared pastry case. | Refrigerate for at least 1 hour, or until firm to the touch. | Beat the cream, cocoa, confectioners' sugar, and amaretto in a large bowl with an electric mixer at high speed until stiff. | Refrigerate for 30 minutes. | Spoon the cream into a pastry bag fitted with a ¾-inch (2-cm) star tip. Pipe rosettes on the top of the mousse in a decorative manner.

white chocolate and lime pie

Serves 6–8 | Prep: 40 min + 4 hr to chill | Cooking:
20 min | Level: 2

For the White Chocolate Filling
1¾ cups (430 ml) heavy (double) cream
6 oz (180 g) best-quality white chocolate,
  coarsely chopped

For the Pastry
¾ cup (125 g) all-purpose (plain) flour
2 teaspoons unsweetened cocoa powder
1 tablespoon confectioners' (icing) sugar
4 tablespoons butter, cut up
1 egg yolk
1–2 tablespoons cold water

4 limes, finely sliced, to decorate

White Chocolate Filling: Heat the cream in a medium saucepan until it just comes to the boil. | Place the chocolate in a large bowl and pour the hot cream over the top. Stir until the chocolate has melted and the mixture is well blended. | Place a sheet of plastic wrap (cling film) on the surface and refrigerate for at least 4 hours. | **Pastry:** Sift the flour, cocoa, and confectioners' sugar into a large bowl. | Use a pastry blender to cut in the butter until the mixture resembles coarse crumbs. | Add the egg yolk and enough water to bind the mixture into a smooth dough. | Press the dough into a disk, wrap in plastic wrap (cling film), and refrigerate for 30 minutes. | Preheat the oven to 400°F (200°C/gas 6). | Set out a 9-inch (23-cm) springform pan. | Roll the pastry out on a lightly floured surface to a 9-inch (23-cm) round. Fit into the pan. | Bake for 15–20 minutes, or until lightly browned. | Let cool completely. | Spoon the filling into the pastry case and decorate with the sliced limes.

pecan chocolate tartlets

Makes about 16 tartlets | Prep: 45 min + 60 min to chill | Cooking: 10 min | Level: 2

For the Pastry
1 cup (150 g) all-purpose (plain) flour
2 tablespoons confectioners' (icing) sugar
4 tablespoons butter
1 egg yolk, lightly beaten
1 tablespoon water

For the Chocolate Cream Filling
½ cup (125 ml) heavy (double) cream
10 oz (300 g) semisweet (dark) chocolate, melted
16 pecan halves, to decorate

Pastry: Sift the flour and confectioners' sugar into a large bowl. | Use your fingertips to rub in the butter until the mixture resembles coarse crumbs. | Add the egg yolk and enough water to form a firm dough. | Press the dough into a disk, wrap in plastic wrap (cling film) and refrigerate for 30 minutes. | Preheat the oven to 350°F (180°C/gas 4). | Set out 8 mini tartlet pans. | Roll the pastry out on a lightly floured surface to ¼ inch (5 mm) thick. | Use a 2-inch (5-cm) cookie cutter to cut out rounds and use them to line the tartlet tins. Prick all over with fork. | Bake for 8–10 minutes, or until lightly browned. | Let cool completely. | Gather the pastry scraps, re-roll, and bake until all the pastry has been used. | **Chocolate Cream Filling**: Heat the cream in a medium saucepan until it just comes to the boil. | Place the chocolate in a large bowl and pour the hot cream over the top. Stir until the chocolate has melted and the mixture is well blended. | Refrigerate until the mixture has a piping consistency. | Spoon the filling into a pastry bag fitted with small fluted tip. | Pipe the filling into the cooled pastry cases. Decorate with the pecans.

cool mint chocolate pie

Serves 6 | Prep: 45 min + 4 hr 30 min to chill | Cooking: 10 min | Level: 3

For the Crumb Base
2 cups (250 g) plain chocolate cookie crumbs
1 cup (150 g) finely ground hazelnuts
½ cup (125 g) butter, melted

For the Chocolate Mint Filling
2 eggs
½ cup (100 g) granulated sugar
⅓ cup (50 g) cornstarch (cornflour) dissolved in 1½ cups (375 ml) milk
7 oz (200 g) semisweet (dark) chocolate, coarsely chopped
1 tablespoon powdered gelatin
4 tablespoons cold water
1 tablespoon mint extract (essence)
1½ cups (310 ml) heavy (double) cream
Fresh raspberries, to decorate
Chocolate shavings, to decorate

Crumb Base: Mix the cookie crumbs, hazelnuts, and butter in a large bowl. Firmly press the mixture into the bottom of a 9-inch (23-cm) springform pan. Refrigerate for 30 minutes. | **Mint Chocolate Filling:** Stir together the eggs and sugar in a double boiler over barely simmering water until the mixture lightly coats a metal spoon or registers 160°F (71°C) on an instant-read thermometer. Immediately plunge the pan into a bowl of ice water and stir until cooled. | Mix in the milk and return to the heat, stirring constantly, until the mixture boils and thickens. | Remove from the heat. Stir in the chocolate until melted. | Sprinkle the gelatin over the water in a double boiler and let soften for 3 minutes. | Place over barely simmering water and cook until the gelatin has dissolved completely. | Add the gelatin to the chocolate mixture and set aside to cool to room temperature. | Mix in the mint extract. | Beat the cream in a large bowl until soft peaks form and fold it into the chocolate mixture. | Spoon the filling into the pan, smoothing the top. Refrigerate for 4 hours before serving. | Decorate with the raspberries and chocolate shavings.

brandy and mincemeat chocolate tart

Serves 6–8 | Prep: 45 min + 30 min to chill | Cooking: 1 hr | Level: 2

Experiment with various decorations to give this tart a personalized finish. Plums in a red wine jus or caramelized grapes are just two suggestions!

For the Pastry
⅔ cup (150 g) butter
¾ cup (150 g) superfine (caster) sugar
3 large eggs
2½ cups (375 g) all-purpose (plain) flour

For the Fruit Mincemeat Filling
1⅔ cups (400 g) fruit mincemeat
1 tablespoon brandy
2 teaspoons very finely chopped lemon zest
2 teaspoons very finely chopped orange zest

For the Chocolate Walnut Frosting
6 tablespoons butter, melted
⅓ cup (70 g) superfine (caster) sugar
⅓ cup (60 g) semisweet (dark) chocolate chips
½ cup (50 g) chopped walnuts
Strawberries, to decorate

Pastry: Place the butter, sugar, and eggs in a food processor and process until just combined. Add the flour to the mixture and process until it forms a dough. | Turn the dough onto a lightly floured surface and knead lightly until smooth. Press the dough into a disk, wrap in plastic wrap (cling film), and refrigerate for 30 minutes. | Preheat the oven to 350°F (180°C/gas 4). | Roll the pastry out until it is large enough to line a 9-inch (23-cm) flan pan. Trim the edges to fit. Line with waxed paper and fill with dried beans or pie weights. | Bake for 8 minutes. Discard the paper with the beans and bake for 8 minutes more. | **Fruit Mincemeat Filling:** Mix the fruit mincemeat, brandy, and lemon and orange zests in a small bowl. | Spread the filling into the pastry case. | Bake for 40–45 minutes, or until firm to the touch. | Let cool completely. | **Chocolate Walnut Frosting:** Melt the butter and sugar in a small saucepan until smooth. Mix in the chocolate chips and walnuts and stir until the chocolate has melted. | Decorate the top of the tart with the strawberries and drizzle with the frosting.

crumbly banana tart

Serves 6–8 | Prep: 45 min + 30 min to chill | Cooking: 45 min | Level: 2

For the Pastry
1⅔ cups (250 g) all-purpose (plain) flour
⅔ cup (100 g) confectioners' (icing) sugar
6 tablespoons butter, cut up
2 eggs, lightly beaten

For the Banana Filling
¾ cup (180 g) butter
¾ cup (150 g) granulated sugar
6 firm-ripe bananas, thinly sliced lengthwise
6 tablespoons heavy (double) cream

For the Cinnamon Streusel Topping
2 tablespoons all-purpose (plain) flour
2 tablespoons dark brown sugar
¼ teaspoon ground cinnamon

Whipped cream, to serve

Pastry: Sift the flour and confectioners' sugar into a large bowl. | Use your fingertips to rub in the butter until the mixture resembles coarse crumbs. | Mix in enough egg to bind the mixture into a smooth dough. | Press the dough into a disk, wrap in plastic wrap (cling film), and refrigerate for 30 minutes. | Preheat the oven to 400°F (200°C/gas 6). | Set out a 8-inch (20-cm) springform pan. | Roll the dough out on a lightly floured surface to a 8-inch (20-cm) round. Fit into the pan. | Bake for 15–20 minutes, or until lightly browned. | Cool completely in the pan. | **Banana Filling:** Cook the butter and sugar in a medium saucepan over medium heat until the sugar has dissolved completely and comes to a boil. Boil for 10 minutes, washing down the sides of the pan with a pastry brush dipped in cold water to prevent sugar crystals from forming. | Mix in the bananas and cream. | Spoon the filling into the pastry case. | **Cinnamon Streusel Topping:** Mix the flour, sugar, and cinnamon and sprinkle over the filling. | Bake for 10–15 minutes, or until lightly browned. | Serve with the whipped cream.

Bars and Brownies

"If you are not feeling well, if you have not slept, chocolate will revive you. But you have no chocolate! I think of that again and again! My dear, how will you ever manage?"
Madame de Sévigné (1626–1696)

cappuccino bars

Makes 22–33 bars | Prep: 30 min | Cooking: 35 min | Level: 1

1½ cups/225 g all-purpose/plain flour
1 teaspoon baking powder
Pinch of salt
2 tablespoons very strong hot coffee
2 tablespoons unsweetened cocoa powder
1 cup/250 g butter, softened
1 cup/200 g granulated sugar
4 large eggs

For the Milk Chocolate Frosting
4 oz/125 g milk chocolate, coarsely chopped
4 tablespoons butter, softened
1 tablespoon milk
1¼ cups/180 g confectioners' (icing) sugar

Preheat the oven to 350°F/180°C/gas 4. | Butter an 11 x 7-inch (28 x 18-cm) baking pan. | Sift the flour, baking powder, and salt into a medium bowl. | Mix the coffee and cocoa in a large bowl. | Add the butter, sugar, eggs, and dry ingredients and beat until well blended. | Pour the batter into the prepared pan. | Bake for 25-35 minutes, or until dry on top and almost firm to the touch. Do not overbake. | Cool completely in the pan. | **Milk Chocolate Frosting**: Melt the chocolate and butter with the milk in a double boiler over barely simmering water. | Remove from the heat and beat in the confectioners' sugar until smooth. | Spread the frosting over the top, letting it run down the sides. Cut into bars.

chocolate and orange squares

Makes 16–25 bars | Prep: 40 min + 1 hr 30 min to chill | Cooking: 35 min | Level: 2

For the Chocolate Cookie Base
1 cup/150 g all-purpose/plain flour
2 tablespoons unsweetened cocoa powder
Pinch of salt
1 cup/250 g butter, softened
⅓ cup/70 g granulated sugar
⅓ cup/50 g confectioners'/icing sugar

For the Orange Filling
Grated zest of 1 orange
½ cup/125 ml fresh orange juice
4 tablespoons water
⅓ cup/50 g cornstarch/cornflour
1 teaspoon fresh lemon juice
1 tablespoon butter, softened
½ cup/160 ml orange marmalade

For the Chocolate Cream Glaze
3 tablespoons heavy/double cream
1½ teaspoons light corn/golden syrup
3 oz/90 g semisweet/dark chocolate,
   coarsely chopped

Preheat the oven to 325°F/170°C/gas 3. | Line an 8-inch (20-cm) baking pan with aluminum foil, letting the edges overhang. | **Chocolate Cookie Base**: Sift the flour, cocoa, and salt into a medium bowl. | Beat the butter, granulated sugar, and confectioners' sugar in a large bowl with an electric mixer at high speed until creamy. | Mix in the dry ingredients. | Firmly press the mixture into the prepared pan to form a smooth, even layer. | Prick all over with a fork. | Bake for 25-30 minutes, or until firm to the touch. | Let cool for 10 minutes. | **Orange Filling**: Mix the orange zest and juice, water, cornstarch, and lemon juice in a small saucepan over medium heat. | Bring to a boil and boil, stirring constantly, for 1 minute, or until thickened. | Remove from the heat and mix in the butter and marmalade until well blended. | Pour the filling evenly over the cookie base. | Bake for 5 minutes. | Cool completely in the pan. | Refrigerate for 1 hour, or until set. | **Chocolate Cream Glaze**: Bring the cream to a boil with the corn syrup in a small saucepan. | Remove from the heat and stir in the chocolate until melted and smooth. | Spoon the glaze into a small freezer bag and cut off a tiny corner. | Pipe over the filling in a decorative manner and refrigerate for 30 minutes. | Transfer to a cutting board and cut into squares.

passionfruit chocolate bars

Makes 16–24 bars | Prep: 30 min + 1 hr to chill | Cooking: 15 min | Level: 2

For the Cookie Base
7 oz (200 g) chocolate cookie crumbs, finely crushed
½ cup (125 g) butter, melted

For the Passionfruit Topping
1 tablespoon powdered gelatin
⅔ cup (150 ml) water
½ cup (100 g) superfine (caster) sugar
2 tablespoons passionfruit pulp
2 oz (60 g) semisweet (dark) chocolate, coarsely chopped

Cookie Base: Butter a deep 8-inch (20-cm) square pan and line the base and sides with aluminum foil. | Mix the cookie crumbs and butter in a large bowl. Press the mixture evenly into the bottom of the prepared pan. | Refrigerate for 30 minutes. | **Passionfruit Topping:** Sprinkle the gelatin over the water in a small saucepan. Let soften for 5 minutes. | Stir in the sugar and place over low heat until the sugar has dissolved completely. Simmer for 5 minutes. | Pour the mixture into a medium bowl and beat with an electric mixer at high speed until white and fluffy. | Use a metal spoon to fold in the passionfruit. | Pour the passionfruit topping over the base, spreading it evenly. | Refrigerate for about 30 minutes, or until set. | Melt the semisweet chocolate in a double boiler over barely simmering water. | Cut into bars. Pipe the chocolate in a loop pattern around the edge of each bar.

nanaimo bars

Makes 36–45 bars | Prep: 30 min + 10 min to freeze + 1 hr to chill | Cooking: 15 min | Level: 2

For the Crumb Base
1 large egg
¼ cup (50 g) granulated sugar
½ cup (125 g) butter
2 cups (250 g) graham cracker or digestive biscuit crumbs
1 cup (120 g) shredded (desiccated) coconut
½ cup (50 g) finely chopped pecans
3 tablespoons unsweetened cocoa powder
1 teaspoon vanilla extract (essence)

For the Vanilla Filling
4 tablespoons butter, softened
3 tablespoons light (single) cream
2¼ cups (330 g) confectioners' (icing) sugar
½ teaspoon vanilla extract (essence)

For the Chocolate Frosting
5 oz (150 g) semisweet (dark) chocolate, coarsely chopped
2 tablespoons butter

Preheat the oven to 350°F (180°C/gas 4). | Butter a 13 x 9-inch (33 x 23-cm) baking pan. | **Crumb Base:** Beat the egg and sugar in a large bowl with an electric mixer at high speed until pale and thick. | Use a wooden spoon to stir in the butter, graham cracker crumbs, coconut, pecans, cocoa, and vanilla. | Firmly press the mixture into the prepared pan to form a smooth, even layer. | Bake for 10-15 minutes, or until firm to the touch. | Let cool completely. | **Vanilla Filling:** Beat the butter, cream, confectioners' sugar, and vanilla in a large bowl with an electric mixer at high speed until well blended. | Spread the mixture over the first layer and freeze for 10 minutes. | **Chocolate Frosting:** Melt the chocolate and butter in a double boiler over barely simmering water. | Spread the frosting over the filling. | Refrigerate for 1 hour, or until set. | Cut into bars.

raspberry chocolate macaroon bars

Makes 36–45 bars | Prep: 25 min | Cooking: 45 min | Level: 1

For the Base
1 cup (150 g) all-purpose (plain) flour
2 tablespoons unsweetened cocoa powder
1/4 teaspoon salt
1/2 cup (125 g) butter, softened
1/2 cup (100 g) granulated sugar
1/2 teaspoon vanilla extract (essence)

For the Chocolate Raspberry Filling
1/2 cup (160 ml) seedless raspberry preserves
1 tablespoon raspberry liqueur
1 cup (180 g) semisweet (dark) chocolate chips
1 1/2 cups (225 g) finely ground almonds
4 large egg whites
1 cup (200 g) granulated sugar
1/2 teaspoon almond extract (essence)
2 tablespoons flaked almonds

Preheat the oven to 325°F (170°C/gas 3). | Line a 13 x 9-inch (33 x 23-cm) baking pan with aluminum foil, letting the edges overhang. | **Base:** Sift the flour, cocoa, and salt into a medium bowl. | Beat the butter, sugar, and vanilla in a large bowl with an electric mixer at high speed until creamy. | Mix in the dry ingredients. | Firmly press the mixture into the prepared pan to form a smooth, even layer. Prick all over with a fork. | Bake for 15–20 minutes, or until firm to the touch. | Increase the oven temperature to 375°F (190°C/gas 5). | **Chocolate Raspberry Filling:** Mix the preserves and liqueur in a small bowl and spread it evenly over the base. Sprinkle with the chocolate chips. | Process the finely ground almonds, egg whites, sugar, and almond extract in a food processor or blender until well blended. | Spoon the mixture over the base and sprinkle with the flaked almonds. | Bake for 20–25 minutes, or until lightly browned. | Transfer to a rack and let cool completely. | Cut into bars.

rich peanut bars

Makes 22–33 bars | Prep: 10 min + 1 hr to chill | Cooking: 10 min | Level: 1

1/2 cup (125 g) butter
2 tablespoons milk
8 oz (250 g) semisweet (dark) chocolate, coarsely chopped
3 cups (450 g) confectioners' (icing) sugar
3/4 cup (75 g) unsalted roasted peanuts, coarsely chopped

Line an 11 x 7-inch (28 x 18-cm) baking pan with aluminum foil. | Mix all the ingredients in a large saucepan. Place over medium heat, stirring constantly, for about 10 minutes, or until the mixture just begins to coat the bottom of the pan. | Spread into the prepared pan and cool completely. | Cover with plastic wrap (cling film) and refrigerate for 1 hour, or until set. | Cut into bars.

no-bake chocolate fruit squares

Makes 16–25 squares | Prep: 15 min + 30 min to chill | Level: 1

½ cup (125 g) butter, cut up
3 tablespoons light corn (golden) syrup
2 tablespoons unsweetened cocoa powder
⅔ cup (120 g) golden raisins (sultanas)
⅓ cup (30 g) candied cherries,
    coarsely chopped
10 oz (300 g) plain, fine-textured cookies,
    broken into small pieces
10 oz (300 g) semisweet (dark) chocolate,
    coarsely chopped

Set out a 9-inch (23-cm) square baking pan. | Melt the butter with the corn syrup and cocoa in a medium saucepan over medium heat. | Stir in the raisins and cherries. | Add the cookies and stir until well mixed. | Spread the mixture evenly in the pan, pressing down lightly. | Melt the chocolate in a double boiler over barely simmering water. Pour the melted chocolate over the cookie mixture. | Refrigerate for 30 minutes, or until the chocolate has set. | Cut into squares.

no-bake choc rum bars

Makes 16–25 squares | Prep: 15 min | Level: 1

8 oz (250 g) chocolate cookie crumbs, crushed
1 cup (180 g) mixed dried fruit
⅓ cup (30 g) chopped walnuts
½ cup (125 g) butter
½ cup (125 ml) sweetened condensed milk
1 teaspoon ground cinnamon
2 tablespoons rum
4 oz (125 g) semisweet (dark) chocolate,
    coarsely chopped

Butter an 8-inch (20-cm) square pan. Line the bottom and sides with aluminum foil. | Mix the cookie crumbs, dried fruit, and walnuts in a large bowl. | Melt the butter with the condensed milk in a small saucepan over low heat. Remove from the heat and add the cinnamon and rum. | Stir the butter mixture into the dry ingredients. | Press the mixture evenly into the prepared pan. | Melt the chocolate in a double boiler over barely simmering water. | Spread the chocolate evenly over the base. | Refrigerate for 30 minutes, or until the chocolate has set. | Cut into squares.

indulgent chocolate brownies

Makes 16–25 squares | Prep: 25 min + 30 min to stand | Cooking: 30 min | Level: 1

1 cup (150 g) all-purpose (plain) flour
1 teaspoon baking powder
Pinch of salt
½ cup (125 g) butter, cut up
6 oz (180 g) bittersweet (plain) chocolate, coarsely chopped
1 cup (200 g) granulated sugar
½ teaspoon vanilla extract (essence)
2 large eggs
½ cup (500 g) coarsely chopped pecans

For the Sour Cream Frosting
3 oz (90 g) bittersweet (plain) chocolate, coarsely chopped
4 tablespoons sour cream
¼ cup (40 g) pecan halves, to decorate

Preheat the oven to 350°F (180°C/gas 4). | Butter an 8-inch (20-cm) baking pan. | Sift the flour, baking powder, and salt into a medium bowl. | Melt the butter and chocolate in a double boiler over barely simmering water. | Transfer to a large bowl and beat in the sugar and vanilla. | Add the eggs, one at a time, beating until just blended. | Mix in the dry ingredients and pecans. | Pour the batter into the prepared pan. | Bake for 25–30 minutes, or until dry on top and almost firm to the touch. Do not overbake. | Cool completely in the pan. | **Sour Cream Frosting**: Melt the chocolate in a double boiler over barely simmering water. | Stir in the sour cream until well blended. | Spread the frosting over the brownie and decorate with the pecan halves. | Let stand for 30 minutes until set. | Cut into squares.

chocolate hazelnut brownies

Makes 16–25 squares | Prep: 15 min | Cooking: 35 min | Level: 1

6 oz (180 g) bittersweet (plain) chocolate
½ cup (125 g) butter
2 large eggs
1 cup (200 g) granulated sugar
⅔ cup (100 g) all-purpose (plain) flour
½ cup (75 g) toasted hazelnuts, peeled and finely chopped
½ teaspoon baking powder
1 teaspoon vanilla extract (essence)
Pinch of salt

Preheat the oven to 350°F (180°C/gas 4). | Butter an 8-inch (20-cm) baking pan and line with waxed paper. | Melt the chocolate with the butter in a double boiler over barely simmering water. Set aside to cool. | Transfer to a large bowl. Add the eggs, one at a time, beating until just blended after just addition. | With mixer at low speed, gradually beat in the sugar, flour, hazelnuts, baking powder, vanilla, and salt. | Spoon the batter into the prepared pan. | Bake for 30–35 minutes, or until dry in top and firm to the touch. Do not overbake. | Cool completely in the pan. | Cut into squares.

date and walnut fudge brownies

Makes 22–33 squares | Prep: 30 min | Cooking: 25 min | Level: 2

1 cup (150 g) all-purpose (plain) flour
1 teaspoon baking powder
Pinch of salt
½ cup (90 g) finely chopped dried dates
½ cup (50 g) chopped walnuts
1 teaspoon grated lemon zest
½ cup (125 g) butter
1 cup (200 g) firmly packed dark brown sugar
2 tablespoons unsweetened cocoa powder
2 tablespoons light corn (golden) syrup
1 egg, lightly beaten
2 oz (60 g) semisweet (dark) chocolate, coarsely chopped
Strawberries, to decorate

Preheat the oven to 350°F (180°C/gas 4). | Butter an 11 x 7-inch (28 x 18-cm) baking pan and line with waxed paper. | Sift the flour, baking powder, and salt into a large bowl. | Mix in the dates, walnuts and lemon zest. | Cook the butter, brown sugar, cocoa, and corn syrup in a small saucepan over low heat, stirring constantly, until the sugar has dissolved completely. | Cool slightly and beat in the egg. | Stir the butter mixture into the dry ingredients until well blended. | Spoon the mixture into the prepared pan, smoothing the surface. | Bake for about 25 minutes, or until a toothpick inserted into the center comes out clean. | Cool completely in the pan. | Melt the chocolate in a double boiler over barely simmering water. | Cut into squares. Drizzle the chocolate over the brownies and top with the strawberries.

double chocolate brownies

Makes 22–33 squares | Prep: 20 min | Cooking: 25 min | Level: 2

1 cup (150 g) all-purpose (plain) flour
1 teaspoon baking powder
Pinch of salt
4 oz (125 g) semisweet (dark) chocolate, coarsely chopped
½ cup (125 g) butter
1¼ cups (250 g) granulated sugar
2 large eggs, lightly beaten
3 oz (90 g) semisweet (dark) chocolate, finely grated

Preheat the oven to 325°F (170°C/gas 3). | Butter an 11 x 7-inch (28 x 18-cm) baking pan and line with parchment paper. | Sift the flour, baking powder, and salt into a medium bowl. | Melt the chopped chocolate with the butter in a double boiler over barely simmering water. | Remove from the heat and beat in the sugar, dry ingredients, and eggs. | Pour the batter into the prepared pan. | Bake for 20-25 minutes, or until dry on top and firm to the touch. Do not overbake. | Sprinkle with the grated chocolate. | Cut into squares.

marbled cream cheese squares

Makes 16–25 squares | Prep: 35 min | Cooking: 30 min | Level: 2

For the Cream Cheese Mixture

1 cup (250 ml) cream cheese, softened

¼ cup (50 g) granulated sugar

2 tablespoons finely grated orange zest

3 tablespoons fresh orange juice

1 teaspoon cornstarch (cornflour)

1 large egg

For the Chocolate Mixture

7 oz (200 g) semisweet (dark) chocolate, coarsely chopped

4 tablespoons cold butter, cut up

¾ cup (150 g) granulated sugar

2 teaspoons vanilla extract (essence)

2 large eggs, lightly beaten with 2 tablespoons cold water

½ cup (75 g) all-purpose (plain) flour

Preheat the oven to 350°F (180°C/gas 4). | Butter a 9-inch (23-cm) square baking pan and line with parchment paper. | **Cream Cheese Mixture:** Beat the cream cheese and sugar in a large bowl with an electric mixer at high speed until creamy. | Beat in the orange zest and juice and cornstarch. | Add the egg, beating until just blended. | **Chocolate Mixture:** Melt the chocolate and butter in a double boiler over barely simmering water. Set aside to cool. | Stir in the sugar and vanilla. | Add the beaten eggs, followed by the flour. | Pour the chocolate mixture into the prepared pan. | Drop tablespoons of the cream cheese mixture over the chocolate base. | Use a thin metal spatula to swirl the mixtures together to create a marbled effect. | Bake for 25–30 minutes, or until slightly risen around the edges and set in the center. | Cool completely in the pan. Cut into bars.

banana brownies

Makes 22–33 bars | Prep: 20 min | Cooking: 35 min | Level: 1

¾ cup (125 g) all-purpose (plain) flour

2 tablespoons unsweetened cocoa powder

1 teaspoon baking powder

Pinch of salt

6 oz (180 g) semisweet (dark) chocolate, coarsely chopped

¾ cup (180 g) butter, softened

1¼ cups (250 g) firmly packed dark brown sugar

1 cup (100 g) coarsely chopped pecans

3 large eggs, lightly beaten

2 firm-ripe bananas, mashed

Preheat the oven to 325°F (170°C/gas 3). | Butter an 11 x 7-inch (28 x 18-cm) baking pan. | Sift the flour, cocoa, baking powder, and salt into a medium bowl. | Melt the chocolate with the butter and brown sugar in a double boiler over barely simmering water until the sugar has dissolved completely. | Remove from the heat and stir in the pecans, eggs, and bananas. | Mix in the dry ingredients. | Spoon the mixture evenly into the prepared pan. | Bake for 25–35 minutes, or until dry on top and firm to the touch. Do not overbake. | Cool completely in the pan. Cut into bars.

Cakes

"I wish for a chocolate cake so dense inside that it is black,
like the devil's ass is blackened by smoke."
Marquis de Sade (1740–1814)

choc roulade

with orange mascarpone cream

Serves 6–8 | Prep: 30 min | Cooking: 20 min | Level: 2

For the Cake
8 oz (250 g) bittersweet (plain) chocolate, coarsely chopped
1½ cups (300 g) granulated sugar
8 large eggs, separated
Pinch of salt

For the Orange Mascarpone Cream
6 large eggs, separated
¾ cup (150 g) granulated sugar
1⅔ cups (400 g) Mascarpone cheese
½ cup (125 ml) orange liqueur

Berryfruit, to decorate

Cake: Preheat the oven to 350°F (180°C/gas 4). | Butter a 15½ x 10½-inch (37 x 27-cm) jelly-roll pan. Line with parchment paper. | Melt the chocolate in a double boiler over barely simmering water. Set aside to cool. | Beat the sugar and egg yolks in a large bowl with an electric mixer at high speed until pale and thick. | With mixer at medium speed, gradually beat in the chocolate. | With mixer at high speed, beat the egg whites and salt in a large bowl until stiff peaks form. | Use a large rubber spatula to fold them into the chocolate mixture. | Spread the batter into the prepared pan. | Bake for 15–20 minutes, or until springy to the touch and a toothpick inserted into the center comes out clean. | Cool the cake in the pan for 5 minutes. | Roll up the cake tightly from the long side. | **Orange Mascarpone Cream:** Beat the egg yolks and ½ cup (100 g) sugar in a large bowl with an electric mixer at high speed until pale and thick. | With mixer at low speed, gradually beat in the Mascarpone and liqueur. Heat gently to 160°F (71°C) | Stir the egg whites and remaining sugar in a saucepan until blended. Stir over low heat, beating constantly, until the whites register 160°F (71°C) on an instant-read thermometer. Transfer to a bowl and beat at high speed until stiff peaks form. Use a large rubber spatula to fold them into the cream. | Unroll the cake and spread with the filling, leaving a 1-inch (2.5-cm) border. | Reroll the cake and decorate with the berryfruit.

walnut

and chocolate cream roll

Serves 6–8 | Prep: 25 min | Cooking: 15 min | Level: 2

For the Cake
6 large egg whites
¼ cup (50 g) granulated sugar
2 large egg yolks, lightly beaten
½ cup (75 g) unsweetened cocoa powder
1 tablespoon all-purpose (plain) flour

1 cup (250 ml) heavy (double) cream

For the Cocoa Frosting
¾ cup (180 g) butter, softened
½ cup (100 g) granulated sugar
½ cup (75 g) unsweetened cocoa powder
¾ cup (75 g) chopped walnuts

Cake: Preheat the oven to 400°F (200°C/gas 6). | Oil a 15 x 10-inch (35 x 25-cm) sheet of parchment paper and place on a baking sheet. | Beat the egg whites in a large bowl with an electric mixer at medium speed until frothy. With mixer at high speed, beat in the sugar, beating until stiff, glossy peaks form. | Use a large rubber spatula to fold in the egg yolks, followed by the cocoa and flour. | Spread the batter into a 9-inch (23-cm) rectangle on the paper. | Bake for 12–15 minutes, or until a toothpick inserted into the center comes out clean. | Cool the cake in the pan for 5 minutes. | Roll up the cake tightly from the long side. | With mixer at high speed, beat the cream in a medium bowl until stiff. | Unroll the cake and spread evenly with the cream, leaving a 1-inch (2.5-cm) border. Reroll the cake and place on a serving plate. | **Cocoa Frosting:** With mixer at high speed, beat the butter and sugar in a medium bowl until creamy. Add the cocoa. | Spread with the frosting. Decorate with the walnuts.

carrot chocolate cake

Serves 6–8 | Prep: 30 min | Cooking: 50 min | Level: 1

For the Carrot Cake

1½ cups (225 g) all-purpose (plain) flour
½ cup (50 g) chopped walnuts
½ cup (90 g) raisins
⅓ cup (45 g) shredded (desiccated)
    sweetened coconut
⅓ cup (50 g) unsweetened cocoa powder
1 teaspoon ground cinnamon
1 teaspoon baking powder
½ teaspoon baking soda
½ teaspoon ground ginger
¼ teaspoon ground nutmeg
Pinch of salt
5 oz (150 g) milk chocolate, coarsely chopped
3 large eggs
¾ cup (150 g) firmly packed brown sugar
½ cup (125 ml) vegetable oil
3 cups (300 g) finely shredded carrots

For the Milk Chocolate Frosting

6 oz (180 g) milk chocolate, coarsely chopped
1 cup (250 ml) cream cheese, softened
2 cups (300 g) confectioners' (icing) sugar

Carrot Cake: Preheat the oven to 350°F (180°C/gas 4). | Butter and flour a 13 x 9-inch (33 x 23-cm) baking pan. | Stir together the flour, walnuts, raisins, coconut, cocoa, cinnamon, baking powder, baking soda, ginger, nutmeg, and salt in a large bowl. | Melt the chocolate in a double boiler over barely simmering water. Set aside to cool. | Beat the eggs, sugar, and oil in a large bowl with an electric mixer at medium speed until creamy. | With mixer at low speed, gradually beat in the dry ingredients, alternating with the chocolate and carrots. | Spoon the batter into the prepared pan. | Bake for 40–50 minutes, or until a toothpick inserted into the center comes out clean. | Cool the cake completely in the pan on a rack. | **Milk Chocolate Frosting:** Melt the chocolate in a double boiler over barely simmering water. Set aside to cool. | With mixer at medium speed, beat the cream cheese and confectioners' sugar in a large bowl. Beat in the melted chocolate. Spread the top of the cake with the frosting.

shortcakes with strawberries and cream

Serves 6–8 | Prep: 30 min + 30 min to chill | Cooking: 20 min | Level: 1

14 oz (400 g) strawberries, hulled and
    thinly sliced
⅓ cup (70 g) + 3 tablespoons sugar
2 tablespoons fresh lemon juice
2 cups (300 g) all-purpose (plain) flour
½ cup (75 g) unsweetened cocoa powder
2 teaspoons baking powder
Pinch of salt
½ cup (125 g) butter, cut up
7 oz (200 g) semisweet (dark) chocolate,
    finely grated
2⅓ cups (580 ml) heavy (double) cream
1 teaspoon vanilla extract (essence)
2 tablespoons confectioners' (icing) sugar

Butter a 12-inch (30-cm) baking sheet and line with parchment paper. | Place the strawberries in a large bowl. Sprinkle with 2 tablespoons sugar and drizzle with the lemon juice. Set aside. | Stir the flour, cocoa, ⅓ cup (70 g) of sugar, baking powder, and salt into a large bowl. | Use your fingertips to rub in the butter until the mixture resembles coarse crumbs. | Stir in 6 oz (180 g) of chocolate, 1¼ cups (310 ml) of cream, and ½ teaspoon vanilla. Mix to form a smooth dough. | Turn the dough out onto a lightly floured surface and knead until smooth. | Press the dough into a disk and roll out to a thickness of 1 inch (3 cm). Cut into an 8-inch (20-cm) rectangle. | Transfer to the prepared baking sheet and refrigerate for 30 minutes. | Preheat the oven to 400°F (200°C/gas 6). | Cut the chilled dough into 9 rectangles and arrange separately on the baking sheet. | Spread each rectangle with a little cream and sprinkle with the remaining sugar. | Bake for 18–20 minutes, or until firm to the touch. | Transfer to racks and let cool completely. | Beat the remaining cream, confectioners' sugar, and ½ teaspoon vanilla in a large bowl with an electric mixer at high speed until stiff. | Slice each cookie horizontally and arrange on individual serving plates. Cover with the strawberry slices and their juices. Top with the cream and the remaining cookie slice. | Sprinkle with the remaining grated chocolate.

chocolate meringue cake

Serves 6–8 | Prep: 25 min | Cooking: 35 min | Level: 2

1 cup (150 g) all-purpose (plain) flour
½ cup (75 g) unsweetened cocoa powder
1 teaspoon baking powder
Pinch of salt
½ cup (125 g) butter, softened
1¼ cups (250 g) granulated sugar
4 large eggs, separated
½ cup (125 ml) buttermilk
½ cup (125 ml) sour cream
2 tablespoons sliced almonds

For the Topping
1 cup (250 ml) heavy (double) cream
2 tablespoons granulated sugar
1 cup (250 g) strawberries,
    hulled and thickly sliced

Preheat the oven to 350°F (180°C/gas 4). | Butter two 9-inch (23-cm) round cake pans. Line with waxed paper. Butter the paper. | Sift the flour, cocoa, baking powder, and salt into a medium bowl. | Beat the butter and ½ cup (100 g) of sugar in a large bowl with an electric mixer at medium speed until creamy. | Add the egg yolks, one at a time, beating until just blended after each addition. | Use a large rubber spatula to fold in the dry ingredients, buttermilk, and sour cream. | Spoon half the batter into each of the prepared pans. | With mixer at medium speed, beat the egg whites in a large bowl until frothy. With mixer at high speed, gradually beat in the remaining sugar, beating until stiff, glossy peaks form. | Spoon the meringue over the batter. Sprinkle the almonds over one of the cakes. | Bake for 10 minutes. Cover loosely with aluminum foil and bake for 25 minutes more. | Remove the foil and cool the cakes in the pans for 5 minutes. Turn out onto racks and carefully remove the paper. Turn meringue-side up and let cool completely. | **Topping**: With mixer at high speed, beat the cream and sugar until stiff. Place the cake without almonds on a serving plate. Spread with the cream and arrange the strawberries on the cream. Top with the remaining cake.

passionfruit layer cake

Serves 6–8 | Prep: 1 hr | Cooking: 1 hr 30 min | Level: 3

5 oz (150 g) white chocolate, chopped
½ cup (125 ml) warm water
1¾ cups (275 g) all-purpose (plain) flour
1 teaspoon baking powder
Pinch of salt
½ cup (125 g) butter
1 cup (200 g) superfine (caster) sugar
2 large eggs
½ cup (125 ml) sour cream

For the Passionfruit Syrup
½ cup (125 ml) water
⅓ cup (70 g) granulated sugar
2 tablespoons strained fresh passionfruit juice

For the Passionfruit Filling
6 tablespoons water
½ cup (100 g) sugar
2 tablespoons strained fresh passionfruit juice
1 cup (250 g) butter
3½ oz (100 g) white chocolate,
    coarsely grated

Preheat the oven to 350°F (180°C/gas 4). | Butter two 8-inch (20-cm) springform pans and line the bottoms with parchment paper. Butter the paper. | Melt the white chocolate with the water in a double boiler over barely simmering water until smooth. Set aside to cool to room temperature. | Sift the flour, baking powder, and salt into a large bowl. | Beat the butter and sugar in a large bowl with an electric mixer at high speed until creamy. | Add the eggs, one at a time, beating until just blended after each addition. | Gradually beat in the chocolate mixture and sour cream. Transfer to a large bowl. | With mixer at low speed, beat in the dry ingredients. | Divide mixture into 8 portions. Spread 1 portion into each of the prepared pans. | Bake for about 10 minutes, or until lightly browned and firm. Cool on racks. | Reline and butter the pans. Repeat with the remaining cake mixture. | **Passionfruit Syrup**: Cook the water and sugar in a small saucepan, stirring constantly over low heat, until the sugar has dissolved completely. Bring to a boil and boil for 1 minute. Let cool and stir in the passionfruit juice. | **Passionfruit Filling**: Cook the water and sugar in a small saucepan, stirring constantly over low heat, until the sugar has dissolved completely. Let cool and stir in the passionfruit juice. | With mixer at high speed, beat the butter in a medium bowl until creamy. Gradually add the cold syrup until well blended. | Place one layer of cake on a serving plate and brush with the syrup. Spread with a thin layer of filling. Repeat with the remaining layers of cake, syrup, and filling. | Spread any remaining filling all over the cake and gently press the grated chocolate around sides.

moist marsala chocolate cake

Serves 6–8 | Prep: 45 min | Cooking: 35 min | Level: 1

For the Cake
1¾ cups (275 g) all-purpose (plain) flour
⅓ cup (50 g) unsweetened cocoa powder
1½ teaspoons baking powder
½ teaspoon baking soda/
   bicarbonate of soda
Pinch of salt
⅔ cup (150 g) butter
1⅓ cups (270 g) granulated sugar
3 large eggs
¾ cup (180 ml) milk
4 tablespoons dry marsala

For the Marsala Cream
1 cup (250 ml) heavy (double) cream
1 tablespoon confectioners' (icing) sugar
1 teaspoon marsala
1 tablespoon unsweetened cocoa powder,
   to dust

Cake: Preheat the oven to 350°F (180°C/gas 4). | Butter an 8-inch (20-cm) square cake pan. Line with waxed paper and butter the paper. | Sift the flour, cocoa, baking powder, baking soda, and salt into a large bowl. | Beat the butter and sugar in a large bowl with an electric mixer at high speed until creamy. | Add the eggs, one at a time, beating until just blended after each addition. | Use a wooden spoon to gradually mix in the dry ingredients and milk until smooth. | Pour the batter into the prepared pan. | Bake for about 45 minutes, or until a toothpick inserted into the center comes out clean. | Brush the hot cake with the marsala. Stand for 5 minutes before turning onto a rack to cool completely. | **Marsala Cream:** Whip the cream with the confectioners' sugar and marsala until stiff. | Spread the cream over the cake and dust with the cocoa.

red velvet cake

Serves 6–8 | Prep: 35 min | Cooking: 30 min | Level: 1

For the Red Velvet Cake
2 cups (300 g) all-purpose (plain) flour
½ cup (75 g) unsweetened cocoa powder
1 teaspoon baking powder
½ teaspoon baking soda/
   bicarbonate of soda
Pinch of salt
½ cup (125 g) butter, softened
1½ cups (300 g) granulated sugar
1 teaspoon vanilla extract (essence)
3 large eggs, at room temperature
1 cup (250 ml) buttermilk
2 tablespoons red food coloring
1 tablespoon white vinegar

For the Vanilla Cream Cheese Frosting
1 cup (250 ml) cream cheese, softened
½ cup (125 g) butter, softened
1 teaspoon vanilla extract (essence)
3 cups (450 g) confectioners' (icing) sugar

Red Velvet Cake: Preheat the oven to 350°F (180°C/gas 4). | Butter two 9-inch (23-cm) round cake pans. Line with waxed paper and butter the paper. | Sift the flour, cocoa, baking powder, baking soda, and salt into a large bowl. | Beat the butter, sugar, and vanilla in a large bowl with an electric mixer at medium speed until creamy. | Add the eggs, one at a time, beating until just blended after each addition. | With mixer at low speed, gradually beat in the dry ingredients, alternating with the buttermilk, food coloring, and vinegar. | Spoon half the batter into each of the prepared pans. | Bake for 25–30 minutes, or until a toothpick inserted into the center comes out clean. | Cool the cakes in the pans for 10 minutes. Turn out onto racks. Carefully remove the paper and let cool completely. | **Vanilla Cream Cheese Frosting:** Beat the cream cheese, butter, and vanilla in a large bowl until creamy. Gradually beat in the confectioners' sugar until fluffy. | Place one cake on a serving plate. Spread with one-third of the frosting. Place the remaining cake on top and spread with the remaining frosting.

chocolate ricotta cake

Serves 8–10 | Prep: 50 min | Cooking: 25 min | Level: 2

For the Cake
1½ cups (225 g) finely ground almonds
⅔ cup (100 g) all-purpose (plain) flour
⅔ cup (100 g) unsweetened cocoa powder
1½ teaspoons baking powder
Pinch of salt
8 large eggs, separated
1½ cups (300 g) granulated sugar
2 teaspoons vanilla extract (essence)
½ teaspoon almond extract (essence)
½ cup (125 ml) milk

For the Ricotta Filling
1 cup (250 ml) heavy (double) cream
2 cups (500 ml) Ricotta cheese
½ cup (75 g) confectioners' (icing) sugar
½ cup (50 g) chopped candied orange peel

For the Chocolate Cream Topping
2 cups (500 ml) heavy (double) cream
⅔ cup (100 g) confectioners' (icing) sugar
⅓ cup (50 g) unsweetened cocoa powder
2 teaspoons vanilla extract (essence)
Shavings of bittersweet chocolate, to decorate

Cake: Preheat the oven to 375°F (190°C/gas 5). | Butter two 9-inch (23-cm) round cake pans. Line with parchment paper. | Stir together the almonds, flour, cocoa, baking powder, and salt in a large bowl. | Beat the egg yolks, 1 cup (200 g) of sugar, and vanilla and almond extracts in a large bowl with an electric mixer at high speed until pale and very thick. | Gradually beat in the dry ingredients, alternating with the milk. | With mixer at medium speed, beat the egg whites in a large bowl until frothy. | With mixer at high speed, gradually beat in the remaining sugar, beating until stiff, glossy peaks form. | Use a large rubber spatula to fold them into the batter. | Spoon half the batter into each of the prepared pans. | Bake for 20–25 minutes, or until a toothpick inserted into the center comes out clean. | Cool the cakes in the pans for 10 minutes. Turn out onto racks. Carefully remove the paper and let cool completely. | **Ricotta Filling:** With mixer at high speed, beat the cream in a medium bowl until stiff. | Process the Ricotta, confectioners' sugar, and orange peel in a food processor until smooth. Transfer to a large bowl. | Use a large rubber spatula to fold the cream into the Ricotta mixture. | **Chocolate Cream Topping:** With mixer at high speed, beat the cream, confectioners' sugar, cocoa, and vanilla in a large bowl until stiff. | Split the cakes horizontally. Place one layer on a serving plate. Spread with one-third of the filling. Repeat with two more cake layers. Place the remaining cake layer on top. | Spread with the topping. Decorate with the chocolate shavings.

viennese walnut torte

Serves 6–8 | Prep: 35 min | Cooking: 60 min | Level: 1

For the Walnut Cake
2¼ cups (330 g) finely ground walnuts
⅓ cup (50 g) all-purpose (plain) flour
½ teaspoon baking powder
¼ teaspoon salt
1 cup (250 g) butter, softened
1¼ cups (250 g) granulated sugar
1 teaspoon vanilla extract (essence)
5 large eggs, separated

For the Chocolate Glaze
5 oz (150 g) semisweet (dark) chocolate, coarsely chopped
½ cup (125 g) butter, softened
2 tablespoons heavy (double) cream (optional)
½ cup (160 ml) orange marmalade

Walnut Cake: Preheat the oven to 350°F (180°C/gas 4). | Butter and flour a 9-inch (23-cm) springform pan. | Stir together the walnuts, flour, baking powder, and salt in a medium bowl. | Beat the butter, half the sugar, and vanilla in a large bowl with an electric mixer at medium speed until creamy. | Add the egg yolks, one at a time, beating until just blended after each addition. | With mixer at medium speed, beat the egg whites in a large bowl until frothy. With mixer at high speed, gradually beat in the remaining sugar until stiff, glossy peaks form. | Use a large rubber spatula to fold them into the batter. Fold in the dry ingredients. | Spoon the batter into the prepared pan. | Bake for 50–60 minutes, or until a toothpick inserted into the center comes out clean. | Cool the cake in the pan for 10 minutes. Loosen and remove the pan sides. Invert onto a rack. Loosen and remove the pan bottom and let cool completely. | **Chocolate Glaze:** Melt the chocolate in a double boiler over barely simmering water. Remove from the heat and gradually stir in the butter until glossy. If needed, stir in the cream. | Split the cake horizontally. Place one layer on a serving plate. Spread with the marmalade. Top with the remaining layer. Drizzle with the glaze.

white chocolate mousse cake with lemon and kiwi

Serves 8–10 | Prep: 1 hr + 12 hr to chill | Level: 2

For the Mousse

6 oz (180 g) white chocolate,
  coarsely chopped
1 cup (250 ml) cream cheese, softened
¼ cup (50 g) granulated sugar
4 teaspoons unflavored gelatin
6 tablespoons fresh orange juice
1½ cups (375 ml) heavy (double) cream

For the Cake

1½ cups (225 g) all-purpose (plain) flour
1½ teaspoons baking powder
Pinch of salt
1 cup (250 g) butter, softened
1 cup (200 g) granulated sugar
2 teaspoons vanilla extract (essence)
4 large eggs, at room temperature
¾ cup (180 ml) milk

For the Lemon Topping

1 teaspoon unflavored gelatin
½ cup (125 ml) fresh lemon juice
¼ cup (50 g) granulated sugar
3-4 medium kiwifruit, peeled and sliced

Mousse: Melt the white chocolate in a double boiler over barely simmering water. Set aside to cool. | Beat the cream cheese and sugar in a large bowl with an electric mixer at medium speed until smooth. | Mix in the white chocolate. | Sprinkle the gelatin over the orange juice in a saucepan. Let stand 1 minute to soften. | Stir over low heat until the gelatin has completely dissolved. Set aside to cool for 30 minutes. | Beat the cooled orange juice into the cream cheese mixture. | With mixer at high speed, beat the cream in a medium bowl until stiff. | Use a rubber spatula to fold the cream into the cream cheese mixture. | **Cake:** Preheat the oven to 350°F (180°C/gas 4). | Butter a 9-inch (23-cm) round cake pan. Line with waxed paper and butter the paper. | Sift the flour, baking powder, and salt into a large bowl. | Beat the butter, sugar, and vanilla in a large bowl with an electric mixer at medium speed until creamy. | Add the eggs, one at a time, beating until just blended after each addition. | With mixer at low speed, gradually beat in the dry ingredients, alternating with the milk. | Spoon the batter into the prepared pan. | Bake for 45-55 minutes, or until a toothpick inserted into the center comes out clean. | Cool in the pan for 10 minutes. Turn out onto a rack. Carefully remove the paper and let cool completely. | Trim the rounded top off the cake. | Return the cake to a 9-inch (23-cm) springform pan. Pour the mousse over the top and refrigerate for 6 hours. | **Lemon Topping:** Sprinkle the gelatin over the lemon juice in a small saucepan. Let stand 1 minute to soften. | Stir in the sugar and cook over low heat until the gelatin has completely dissolved. Remove from the heat and set aside to cool. | Pour the topping over the mousse and refrigerate for 6 hours, or until set. | Loosen and remove the pan sides. Decorate with the kiwifruit.

double chocolate angel food cake

Serves 8–10 | Prep: 20 min | Cooking: 1 hr | Level: 2

¾ cup (125 g) all-purpose (plain) flour
2 tablespoons unsweetened cocoa powder
1 cup (200 g) superfine (caster) sugar
12 large egg whites
1 teaspoon cream of tartar
Pinch of salt
1 teaspoon vanilla extract (essence)
4 tablespoons chocolate syrup
  (the best option is ice-cream syrup in a
  plastic squeeze bottle)

Preheat the oven to 325°F (170°C/gas 3). | Set out a 10-inch (25-cm) tube pan with a removable bottom. | Sift the flour and cocoa powder into a large bowl. Stir in ½ cup (100 g) of sugar. | Beat the egg whites, cream of tartar, and salt in a large bowl with an electric mixer at medium speed until frothy. | With mixer at high speed, gradually beat in the remaining sugar, beating until stiff peaks form. Add the vanilla. | Use a large rubber spatula to gradually fold in the dry ingredients. | Spoon one-third of the batter into the pan. Drizzle with half the chocolate syrup. Use a spoon to swirl the syrup and batter together. Spoon another one-third of the batter over and drizzle with the remaining syrup. Swirl the syrup and batter once more. Top with the remaining batter. | Bake for 50-60 minutes, or until golden brown and springy to the touch. | Cool the cake completely over a heatproof bottle or pudding mold.

cantaloupe gâteau

Serves 6–8 | Prep: 40 min + 3 hr to chill | Cooking: 40 min | Level: 2

For the Cake

4 oz (125 g) bittersweet (dark) chocolate
1⅓ cups (200 g) all-purpose (plain) flour
⅓ cup (50 g) unsweetened cocoa powder
1 teaspoon baking powder
Pinch of salt
½ cup (125 g) butter, softened
¾ cup (150 g) granulated sugar
3 large eggs, separated

For the Filling

½ ripe cantaloupe, seeded
3 large egg yolks
6 tablespoons milk
½ cup (100 g) granulated sugar
1 tablespoon unflavored gelatin
4 tablespoons water
2 cups (500 ml) heavy (double) cream, whipped
Shavings of bittersweet (dark) chocolate, to decorate

Cake: Preheat the oven to 350°F (180°C/gas 4). | Butter a 9-inch (23-cm) round cake pan. | Melt the chocolate in a double boiler over barely simmering water. | Sift the flour, cocoa, baking powder, and salt into a medium bowl. | Beat the butter and sugar in a large bowl with an electric mixer at medium speed until creamy. | Add the egg yolks, one at a time, beating until just blended after each addition. | Gradually beat in the chocolate and the dry ingredients. | Beat the egg whites in a medium bowl until stiff peaks form. Fold them into the batter. | Spoon the batter into the prepared pan. | Bake for 35–40 minutes, or until a toothpick inserted into the center comes out clean. | Turn out onto a rack to cool completely. | **Filling**: Cut the cantaloupe half into 2 pieces. Peel one piece with a knife and cut into chunks. Puree the melon chunks until smooth. Slice the remaining melon very thinly, reserving any juice. Refrigerate the puree, melon slices, and juice. | Beat the egg yolks, milk, and sugar in a medium saucepan. Cook over low heat, stirring constantly with a wooden spoon, until the mixture registers 160°F (71°C) on an instant-read thermometer. Immediately plunge the pan into a bowl of ice water and stir until cooled. Beat until thick. | Sprinkle the gelatin over the water in a saucepan. Place over low heat and stir until completely dissolved. | Stir the gelatin and pureed cantaloupe into the egg mixture. Fold in the whipped cream. | Split the cake horizontally. Place one layer in a 10-inch (25-cm) springform pan. | Drizzle with some reserved juice and spread with half the cantaloupe filling. Place the remaining layer on top. Drizzle with the cantaloupe juice and spread the remaining filling over the top and down onto the sides. | Decorate with the cantaloupe slices and the chocolate shavings. | Refrigerate for 3 hours. Loosen and remove the pan sides.

mocha cake with chantilly cream

Serves 6–8 | Prep: 25 min | Cooking: 35 min | Level: 2

For the Cake

1 cup (150 g) all-purpose (plain) flour
2 tablespoons unsweetened cocoa powder
1 teaspoon baking powder
Pinch of salt
4 large eggs, separated
¾ cup (150 g) granulated sugar
4 tablespoons milk

For the Chantilly Cream

2 cups (500 ml) heavy (double) cream
¼ cup (50 g) granulated sugar

For the Mocha Frosting

2½ cups (375 g) confectioners' (icing) sugar
4 tablespoons unsweetened cocoa powder
2 tablespoons butter, melted
1 tablespoon freeze-dried coffee granules dissolved in 2 tablespoons hot water

Cake: Preheat the oven to 375°F (190°C/gas 5). | Butter two 8-inch (20-cm) round cake pans. Line with parchment paper. | Sift the flour, cocoa, baking powder, and salt onto a sheet of paper. | Beat the egg yolks and sugar in a large bowl with an electric mixer at high speed until pale and thick. | With mixer at low speed, gradually beat in the dry ingredients, alternating with the milk. | With mixer at high speed, beat the egg whites in a large bowl until stiff peaks form. Use a large rubber spatula to fold them into the batter. | Spoon half the batter into each of the prepared pans. | Bake for 25–35 minutes, or until springy to the touch and a toothpick inserted into the center comes out clean. | Cool in the pans for 5 minutes. Turn out onto racks. Carefully remove the paper and let cool completely. | **Chantilly Cream**: Beat the cream and sugar in a large bowl until stiff. | **Mocha Frosting**: Beat the confectioners' sugar, cocoa, butter, and coffee mixture in a medium bowl to make a spreadable frosting. | Place one cake on a serving plate and spread with the chantilly cream. Top with the remaining cake. Spread the top of the cake with the frosting.

almond berry supreme

Serves 10–12 | Prep: 1 hr | Cooking: 1 hr 40 min | Level: 3

3 cups (450 g) all-purpose (plain) flour

2 teaspoons baking powder

½ teaspoon baking soda/bicarbonate of soda

½ teaspoon salt

2 cups (300 g) finely ground almonds

2 cups (500 g) butter, softened

4 cups (800 g) granulated sugar

12 large eggs, at room temperature

1¼ cups (310 ml) sour cream

1¼ cups (310 g) fresh or frozen and
thawed raspberries

1¼ cups (310 g) fresh or frozen and
thawed blackberries

2 cups (500 ml) White Chocolate Ganache
(see page 152)

5 oz (150 g) white chocolate,
coarsely chopped

10 oz (300 g) semisweet (dark) chocolate,
coarsely chopped

2⅔ cups (650 g) mixed fresh berries, grapes,
and fresh currants

Preheat the oven to 350°F (180°C/gas 4). | Butter one 10 x 3-inch (25 x 8-cm) and one 7 x 3-inch (18 x 8-cm) round cake pans. Line with waxed paper. Butter the paper. | Sift the flour, baking powder, baking soda, and salt into a large bowl. Add the almonds. | Beat the butter and sugar in a large bowl with an electric mixer at medium speed until creamy. | Add the eggs, one at a time, beating until just blended after each addition. | Gradually beat in the dry ingredients, alternating with the sour cream, raspberries, and blackberries. | Spoon three-quarters of the batter into the prepared 10-inch (25-cm) pan. Spoon the remaining batter into the 7-inch (18-cm) pan. | Bake the 10-inch cake for about 1 hour and 30–40 minutes, or until a toothpick inserted into the center comes out clean. Bake the 7-inch cake for 50–60 minutes, or until a toothpick inserted into the center comes out clean. | Cool in the pans for 5 minutes. Turn out onto racks and carefully remove the paper. Let cool completely. | Place the large cake on a serving plate. Spread with two-thirds of the ganache. Center the smaller cake on top. Spread with the remaining ganache. | Melt the white chocolate in a double boiler over barely simmering water. Set aside. | Melt the dark chocolate in a double boiler over barely simmering water. Set aside. | Cut 1 strip of parchment paper to measure 2½ x 27½ inches (6 x 70-cm). Cut another strip to measure 3½ x 40 inches (9 x 100-cm). Cut a wave pattern ½-inch (1-cm) from the top. Spread the short strip with the white chocolate. Spread the long strip with the dark chocolate. Wrap the smaller strip around the top layer of cake. Wrap the larger strip around the bottom layer. Set aside. Carefully remove the paper. | Decorate with the fruit.

spiced italian fruit cake with chocolate glaze

Serves 8–10 | Prep: 1 hr | Cooking: 30 min | Level: 1

½ cup (50 g) chopped walnuts

¼ cup (25 g) chopped almonds

¼ cup (25 g) chopped hazelnuts

¼ cup (30 g) pine nuts

⅔ cup (70 g) mixed candied orange and lemon
peel, cut into small cubes

2 tablespoons raisins

⅓ cup (50 g) unsweetened cocoa powder

3 oz (90 g) semisweet (dark) chocolate,
chopped

½ teaspoon ground cinnamon

½ teaspoon ground nutmeg

½ teaspoon ground coriander

½ teaspoon ground black pepper

¼ cup (60 g) honey, warmed

2⅓ cups (350 g) all-purpose (plain) flour

¼ teaspoon fennel seeds

½ cup (125 ml) boiling water

12 oz (300 g) semisweet (dark) chocolate,
coarsely chopped, to glaze

Preheat the oven to 325°F (170°C/gas 3). | Butter and flour a 10-inch (25-cm) round cake pan. | Mix together the walnuts, almonds, hazelnuts, pine nuts, candied peel, raisins, cocoa, chocolate, cinnamon, nutmeg, coriander, and pepper in a large bowl. Stir in the honey, flour, and fennel seeds. Add the water and mix well. | Spoon the batter into the prepared pan. | Bake for 25–30 minutes, or until light golden brown. | Cool the cake in the pan for 30 minutes. Turn out onto a rack to cool completely. | Melt the chocolate in a double boiler over barely simmering water. Set aside to cool for 10 minutes. Spread the chocolate over the cake.

chocolate cherry sponge

chocolate

Serves 6–8 | Prep: 1 hr | Cooking: 1 hr | Level: 2

For the Chocolate Cake
9 oz (275 g) bittersweet (plain) chocolate,
  coarsely chopped
2 cups (300 g) all-purpose (plain) flour
⅓ cup (50 g) unsweetened cocoa powder
2 teaspoons baking powder
½ teaspoon baking soda/
  bicarbonate of soda
Pinch of salt
1 cup (250 g) butter, softened
2½ cups (500 g) granulated sugar
4 large eggs, at room temperature
½ cup (125 ml) milk
2 tablespoons vegetable oil

14 oz (400 g) bittersweet (dark) chocolate,
  coarsely chopped
1 cup (250 ml) heavy (double) cream
1¼ cups (310 g) canned sour cherries,
  drained (reserve the juice)
1 tablespoon kirsch or other cherry liqueur
Grated chocolate, to decorate

Chocolate Cake: Preheat the oven to 350°F (180°C/gas 4). | Butter and flour a 9-inch (23-cm) springform pan. | Melt the chocolate in a double boiler over barely simmering water. | Sift the flour, cocoa, baking powder, baking soda, and salt into a large bowl. | Beat the butter and sugar in a large bowl with an electric mixer at medium speed until creamy. | Add the eggs, one at a time, beating until just blended after each addition. | Gradually beat in the dry ingredients, alternating with the chocolate, milk, and oil. | Spoon the batter into the prepared pan. | Bake for 50–60 minutes, or until a toothpick inserted into the center comes out clean. | Cool in the pan for 10 minutes. Loosen and remove the pan sides and cool completely. | Place the chocolate in a medium bowl. | Bring the cream to a boil in a small saucepan over medium heat. Pour the cream over the chocolate. Cover and let stand until it starts to melt. Stir vigorously and set aside to cool. | Beat until glossy. | Mix the reserved cherry juices and the kirsch in a small bowl. | Split the cake in three horizontally. Place one layer on a serving plate. | Drizzle with the kirsch mixture. Spread with a quarter of the chocolate cream and top with cherries. Top with another layer. Drizzle with the kirsch, spread with chocolate cream, and top with the remaining cherries. Place the remaining layer on top. Spread with the remaining chocolate cream. | Decorate with the grated chocolate.

chocolate and banana cake with cream cheese frosting

Serves 6–8 | Prep: 20 min | Cooking: 40 min | Level: 1

For the Cake
2 cups (300 g) all-purpose (plain) flour
½ cup (75 g) unsweetened cocoa powder
1½ teaspoons baking powder
½ teaspoon baking soda/bicarbonate of soda
Pinch of salt
1 cup (200 g) granulated sugar
2 large eggs, at room temperature
¾ cup (180 ml) hot water
1 cup (250 g) mashed very ripe bananas
  (about 3 large bananas)
1½ teaspoons vanilla extract (essence)

For the Cream Cheese Frosting
7 tablespoons cream cheese, softened
4 tablespoons butter, softened
1 teaspoon vanilla extract (essence)
2 cups (300 g) confectioners' (icing) sugar
2 tablespoons unsweetened cocoa powder

Cake: Preheat the oven to 350°F (180°C/gas 4). | Butter a 9-inch (23-cm) square baking pan. Line with waxed paper and butter the paper. | Sift the flour, cocoa, baking powder, baking soda, and salt into a large bowl. Stir in the sugar. | Beat in the eggs, water, bananas, and vanilla. | Spoon the batter into the prepared pan. | Bake for 35–40 minutes, or until a toothpick inserted into the center comes out clean. | Cool in the pan for 10 minutes. | Turn out onto a rack. Carefully remove the paper and let cool completely. | **Cream Cheese Frosting:** Beat the cream cheese, butter, and vanilla in a large bowl until creamy. Beat in the confectioners' sugar and cocoa. | Spread the cake with the frosting.

layer cake with fresh figs

Serves 6–8 | Prep: 45 min | Cooking: 1 hr | Level: 1

For the Chocolate Cake
9 oz (275 g) bittersweet (dark) chocolate,
    coarsely chopped
2 cups (300 g) all-purpose (plain) flour
⅓ cup (50 g) unsweetened cocoa powder
2 teaspoons baking powder
½ teaspoon baking soda/bicarbonate of soda
Pinch of salt
1 cup (250 g) butter, softened
2½ cups (500 g) granulated sugar
4 large eggs, at room temperature
½ cup (125 ml) milk
2 tablespoons vegetable oil

For the Chocolate Filling
1 cup (250 g) butter, softened
⅓ cup (50 g) unsweetened cocoa powder
⅓ cup (50 g) confectioners' (icing) sugar
1 teaspoon vanilla extract (essence)
½ cup (125 ml) orange liqueur
½ cup (160 ml) raspberry preserves
12 oz (300 g) bittersweet (dark) chocolate,
    coarsely chopped
8 fresh green or black figs,
    stemmed and halved

Chocolate Cake: Preheat the oven to 350°F (180°C/gas 4). | Butter and flour a 9-inch (23-cm) springform pan. | Melt the chocolate in a double boiler over barely simmering water. | Sift the flour, cocoa, baking powder, baking soda, and salt into a large bowl. | Beat the butter and sugar in a large bowl with an electric mixer at medium speed until creamy. | Add the eggs, one at a time, beating until just blended after each addition. | Gradually beat in the dry ingredients, alternating with the chocolate, milk, and oil. | Spoon the batter into the prepared pan. | Bake for 50–60 minutes, or until a toothpick inserted into the center comes out clean. | Cool in the pan for 10 minutes. Loosen and remove the pan sides and cool completely. | **Chocolate Filling:** Beat the butter in a large bowl with an electric mixer at medium speed until creamy. | Gradually beat in the cocoa, confectioners' sugar, and vanilla until creamy. | Split the cake in three horizontally. | Place one layer on a serving plate. Drizzle with a little liqueur and spread with the preserves. Spread with a layer of the filling. Top with another layer. Repeat until all the layers, liqueur, preserves, and filling are used, finishing with a cake layer topped with filling. | Melt the chocolate in a double boiler over barely simmering water. | Cover a work surface with waxed paper and use a pencil to mark on about twenty-five 2 x 5-inch (5 x 13-cm) strips. Turn the paper over. | Use a metal spatula to spread the melted chocolate to fit into the marked strips. Set aside to cool. | Trim one end of the chocolate strips so that they are the same height as the cake, and arrange them around the sides of the cake, slightly overlapping each strip. | Arrange the figs on the top of the cake.

fudge sundae cake

Serves 6–8 | Prep: 25 min | Cooking: 55 min | Level: 1

1⅔ cups (250 g) all-purpose (plain) flour
1 cup (150 g) unsweetened cocoa powder
1½ teaspoons baking powder
Pinch of salt
1¼ cups (250 g) granulated sugar
1 cup (250 ml) milk
6 tablespoons butter, melted
2 teaspoons vanilla extract (essence)
1 cup (100 g) chopped walnuts or pecans
1¾ cups (350 g) firmly packed brown sugar
2½ cups (625 ml) boiling water

Preheat the oven to 350°F (180°C/gas 4). | Butter a 13 x 9-inch (33 x 23-cm) baking pan. | Sift the flour, ½ cup (75 g) of cocoa, baking powder, and salt into a large bowl. Stir in the sugar. | Mix the milk, butter, and vanilla in a medium bowl. Beat the milk mixture into the dry ingredients with an electric mixer at low speed. | Stir in the nuts. | Spoon the batter into the prepared pan. Place the pan on a baking sheet. Mix the brown sugar and remaining cocoa in a medium bowl. Sprinkle over the batter and pour the water carefully over the cake. | Bake for 45–55 minutes, or until a toothpick inserted into the center comes out clean. | Serve the cake from the pan while still warm, spooning a little of the sauce that forms in the bottom of the pan over each serving.

chocolate applesauce cake

Serves 4–6 | Prep: 20 min | Cooking: 35 min | Level: 1

1 cup (150 g) all-purpose (plain) flour
2 tablespoons unsweetened cocoa powder
¾ teaspoon baking soda/bicarbonate of soda
Pinch of salt
4 tablespoons butter, softened
¾ cup (150 g) granulated sugar
1 teaspoon vanilla extract (essence)
2 large eggs, at room temperature
1 cup (250 ml) unsweetened applesauce
½ cup (90 g) semisweet (dark)
   chocolate chips
½ cup (50 g) chopped walnuts

Preheat the oven to 350°F (180°C/gas 4). | Butter and flour an 8-inch (20-cm) square baking pan. | Sift the flour, cocoa, baking soda, and salt into a medium bowl. | Beat the butter, sugar, and vanilla in a large bowl with an electric mixer at medium speed until creamy. | Add the eggs, one at a time, beating until just blended after each addition. | With mixer at low speed, gradually beat in the dry ingredients, alternating with the applesauce. | Spoon the batter into the prepared pan. Sprinkle with the chocolate chips and walnuts. | Bake for 30–35 minutes, or until a toothpick inserted into the center comes out clean. | Cool completely in the pan on a rack.

layer cake with truffles

Serves 6–8 | Prep: 45 min + 30 min to chill | Cooking: 35 min | Level: 3

For the Truffles
4 oz (125 g) bittersweet (dark) chocolate,
   coarsely chopped
3 tablespoons heavy (double) cream
1 tablespoon butter
⅓ cup (50 g) confectioners' (icing) sugar
2 tablespoons orange liqueur
⅓ cup (50 g unsweetened cocoa powder
   (optional)

For the Cake
2 cups (300 g) all-purpose (plain) flour
2 tablespoons unsweetened cocoa powder
1 teaspoon baking powder
½ teaspoon baking soda/bicarbonate of soda
Pinch of salt
2 oz (60 g) semisweet (dark) chocolate,
   chopped
6 tablespoons butter, softened
¾ cup (150 g) granulated sugar
7 tablespoons cream cheese, softened
2 large eggs, at room temperature
1 tablespoon orange liqueur
1 teaspoon vanilla extract (essence)
¾ cup (180 ml) water

For the Filling
8 oz (250 g) semisweet (dark) chocolate,
   chopped
6 tablespoons heavy (double) cream

Truffles: Melt the chocolate, cream, and butter in a double boiler over barely simmering water. Stir in the confectioners' sugar and orange liqueur until smooth. | Roll spoonfuls of the mixture into marble-sized balls, dusting your hands with cocoa, if needed. Transfer to a plate and refrigerate for 30 minutes. | **Cake:** Preheat the oven to 350°F (180°C/gas 4). | Butter two 9-inch (23-cm) springform pans. | Sift the flour, cocoa, baking powder, baking soda, and salt into a large bowl. | Melt the chocolate in a double boiler over barely simmering water. Set aside to cool. | Beat the butter, sugar, and cream cheese in a large bowl with an electric mixer at medium speed until creamy. | Add the eggs, one at a time, beating until just blended after each addition. | With mixer at low speed, gradually beat in the chocolate, orange liqueur, and vanilla. Beat in the dry ingredients, alternating with the water. | Spoon half the batter into each of the prepared pans. | Bake for 25–35 minutes, or until a toothpick inserted into the centers comes out clean. | Cool in the pans for 10 minutes. Loosen and remove the pan sides. Invert onto racks. Loosen and remove the pan bottoms. | **Filling:** Melt the chocolate and cream in a double boiler over barely simmering water. Set aside to cool. | Split each cake horizontally. Place one layer on a serving plate. Spread with one-third of the filling. Repeat with 2 more cake layers. Top with the remaining layer. | Spread the cake with the remaining filling. Decorate with the truffles.

chocolate orange marble cake

Serves 6–8 | Prep: 30 min | Cooking: 45 min | Level: 1

For the Marble Cake
2 cups (300 g) all-purpose (plain) flour
2 teaspoons baking powder
Pinch of salt
2½ oz (50 g) bittersweet (dark) chocolate,
   coarsely chopped
½ cup (125 g) butter, softened
1½ cups (300 g) granulated sugar
2 teaspoons vanilla extract (essence)
2 large eggs, at room temperature
¾ cup (180 ml) milk
2 tablespoons grated orange zest

For the Fudge Frosting
4 oz (125 g) bittersweet (plain) chocolate,
   coarsely chopped
½ cup (125 g) butter, softened
3½ cups (525 g) confectioners' (icing) sugar
4 tablespoons milk
1 teaspoon vanilla extract (essence)
Candied orange slices, to decorate

Marble Cake: Preheat the oven to 350°F (180°C/gas 4). | Butter two 9-inch (23-cm) round cake pans. Line with waxed paper and butter the paper. | Sift the flour, baking powder, and salt into a large bowl. | Melt the chocolate in a double boiler over barely simmering water. Set aside to cool. | Beat the butter, sugar, and vanilla in a large bowl with an electric mixer at medium speed until creamy. | Add the eggs, one at a time, beating until just blended after each addition. | Gradually beat in the dry ingredients, alternating with the milk. | Place half the batter in another bowl. Stir the chocolate into one bowl of batter and the orange zest into the other. | Drop alternating spoonfuls of the batters into the pans. Swirl the batters together with a knife to create a marbled effect. | Bake for 35–45 minutes, or until a toothpick inserted into the center comes out clean. | Cool the cakes in the pans for 10 minutes. | Turn out onto racks. Carefully remove the paper and let cool completely. | **Fudge Frosting:** Melt the chocolate in a double boiler over barely simmering water. Set aside to cool. | With mixer at high speed, beat the butter and half the confectioners' sugar in a large bowl until creamy. Beat in the chocolate, milk, and vanilla. Beat in the remaining confectioners' sugar. | Place one cake on a serving plate. Spread with one-third of the frosting. Top with the remaining cake. Spread the top and sides with the remaining frosting. Decorate with the candied orange slices.

sour cream cake with cherry liqueur cream

Serves 6–8 | Prep: 30 min | Cooking: 55 min | Level: 2

For the Cake
1⅔ cups (250 g) all-purpose (plain) flour
1½ teaspoons baking powder
Pinch of salt
5 oz (150 g) semisweet (dark) chocolate,
   coarsely chopped
½ cup (125 ml) water
½ cup (125 g) butter, softened
1¼ cups (250 g) firmly packed brown sugar
2 large eggs, at room temperature
½ cup (125 ml) sour cream

For the Cherry Liqueur Cream
1½ cups (485 ml) cherry jam or preserves
3 tablespoons kirsch
2 cups (500 ml) heavy (double) cream

For the Chocolate Frosting
8 oz (250 g) bittersweet (plain) chocolate,
   coarsely chopped
2 tablespoons butter
Candied cherries, to decorate

Cake: Preheat the oven to 350°F (180°C/gas 4). | Butter two 9-inch (23-cm) round cake pans. Line with waxed paper and butter the paper. | Sift the flour, baking powder, and salt into a large bowl. | Melt the chocolate and water in a double boiler over barely simmering water. | Beat the butter and brown sugar in a large bowl with an electric mixer at medium speed until creamy. | Add the eggs, one at a time, beating until just blended after each addition. | Gradually beat in the chocolate mixture, sour cream, and dry ingredients. | Spoon half the batter into each of the prepared pans. | Bake for 45–55 minutes, or until a toothpick inserted into the centers comes out clean. | Cool the cakes in the pans for 10 minutes. Turn out onto racks. Carefully remove the waxed paper and let cool completely. | Split the cakes horizontally. | **Cherry Liqueur Cream:** Mix the jam with the kirsch in a small bowl. | With mixer at high speed, beat the cream in a medium bowl until stiff. | **Chocolate Frosting:** Melt the chocolate and butter in a double boiler over barely simmering water. | Place one layer on a serving plate. Spread with one-third of the jam mixture and one-third of the cream. Repeat with the remaining cake layers, finishing with a plain layer. Spread the frosting over the top and sides of the cake. | Decorate with the candied cherries.

dobos torte

Serves 6–8 | Prep: 1 hr 15 min | Cooking: 30 min | Level: 3

This famous Hungarian cake was created by master chef Jósef Dobos in the second half of the 19th century. He presented it officially at a national show in 1885. No one else quite got it right until 1906, when chef Dobos finally released the recipe.

For the Cake Layers
1 cup (150 g) all-purpose (plain) flour
Pinch of salt
6 large eggs, separated
1½ cups (225 g) confectioners' (icing) sugar
1 teaspoon vanilla extract (essence)

For the Chocolate Buttercream
5 oz (150 g) bittersweet ((dark) chocolate, coarsely chopped
1¾ cups (430 g) butter, softened
1½ cups (225 g) confectioners' (icing) sugar
2 tablespoons unsweetened cocoa powder
1 teaspoon vanilla extract (essence)

For the Caramel Glaze
1 cup (200 g) granulated sugar
3 tablespoons water
1 tablespoon butter
2 teaspoons fresh lemon juice
10 whole, toasted and peeled hazelnuts

Cake Layers: Preheat the oven to 350°F (180°C/gas 4). | Butter two 9-inch (23-cm) round cake pans. Line with parchment paper. | Sift the flour and salt into a medium bowl. Beat the egg yolks, ¾ cup (125 g) of confectioners' sugar, and vanilla in a large bowl with an electric mixer at high speed until pale and very thick. | Beat the egg whites in a large bowl until frothy. With mixer at high speed, gradually beat in the remaining confectioners' sugar, beating until stiff, glossy peaks form. Use a large rubber spatula to fold them into the batter. Fold in the dry ingredients. | Spoon ⅔ cup (150 ml) of batter into each of the prepared pans. | Bake for 5–8 minutes, or until golden brown. | Cool in the pans for 5 minutes. Turn out onto racks. Carefully remove the paper and let cool completely. Cool and clean the pans, butter and flour them, and reline with paper. Repeat until all the batter is used up, making 6 or 7 layers. | **Chocolate Buttercream:** Melt the chocolate in a double boiler over barely simmering water. | Beat the butter in a large bowl until creamy. Add the confectioners' sugar, cocoa, chocolate, and vanilla. | Place one layer on a serving plate and spread with some buttercream. Repeat with all but the top layer. Place this layer on a large plate. Spread the cake with the remaining buttercream. | **Caramel Glaze:** Bring the sugar, water, butter, and lemon juice to a boil in a saucepan over medium heat, until the sugar has dissolved. Boil until the mixture is amber colored. | Spread the caramel over the reserved cake layer. Set for about 30 seconds. Use a sharp knife to cut the layer into 10 equal, wedge-shaped portions. Let cool completely. | Using the whole hazelnuts as props, arrange the wedges of cake on top of the cake overlapping, and each on an angle, to resemble the photograph.

mud cake with white chocolate ganache and walnuts

Serves 6–8 | Prep: 30 min | Cooking: 70 min | Level: 1

1 cup (200 g) firmly packed brown sugar
1 cup (250 ml) milk
¾ cup (180 g) butter, cut up
6 tablespoons molasses (treacle)
5 oz (150 g) white chocolate, coarsely chopped
2 cups (300 g) all-purpose (plain) flour
2 teaspoons baking powder
Pinch of salt
2 large eggs, lightly beaten
1½ cups (375 ml White Chocolate Ganache (see page 152)
12 walnut halves

Preheat the oven to 325°F (170°C/gas 3). | Butter a 9-inch (23-cm) round cake pan. Line with waxed paper. | Place the brown sugar, milk, butter, molasses, and chocolate in a saucepan and stir over low heat, without boiling, until smooth. Set aside to cool. | Sift the flour, baking powder, and salt into a medium bowl. Gradually stir the dry ingredients and eggs into the sugar mixture. | Spoon the batter into the prepared pan. | Bake for 60–70 minutes, or until a toothpick inserted into the center comes out clean. | Cool the cake completely in the pan. Turn out onto a rack. Carefully remove the paper and let cool completely. | Spread with the ganache and decorate with the walnuts.

lime and white chocolate bundt cake

Serves 6–8 | Prep: 20 min | Cooking: 50 min | Level: 1

5 oz (150 g) white chocolate,
  coarsely chopped
2 cups (300 g) all-purpose (plain) flour
2 teaspoons baking powder
Pinch of salt
1 cup (250 g) butter, softened
½ cup (100 g) granulated sugar
1–2 tablespoons grated lime zest
3 large eggs, separated
4 tablespoons milk

For the Lime Frosting
1 cup (150 g) confectioners' (icing) sugar
1 tablespoon butter, melted
1 tablespoon grated lime zest
1–2 tablespoons fresh lime juice

Preheat the oven to 350°F (180°C/gas 4). | Butter and flour a 9-inch (23-cm) Bundt pan. | Melt the chocolate in a double boiler over barely simmering water. Set aside to cool. | Sift the flour, baking powder, and salt into a medium bowl. | Beat the butter, sugar, and lime zest in a large bowl with an electric mixer at medium speed until creamy. | Add the egg yolks, one at a time, beating until just blended after each addition. | Gradually beat in the chocolate, followed by the dry ingredients, alternating with the milk. | With mixer at high speed, beat the egg whites in a medium bowl until stiff peaks form. Use a large rubber spatula to fold them into the batter. | Spoon the batter into the prepared pan. | Bake for 40–50 minutes, or until a toothpick inserted into the center comes out clean. | Cool the cake in the pan for 10 minutes. Turn out onto a rack to cool completely. | **Lime Frosting:** Mix the confectioners' sugar, butter, and lime zest in a large bowl. Beat in enough lime juice to make a thick, spreadable frosting. Pour the frosting over the top of the cake, letting it drip down the sides.

frosted chocolate cake

Serves 6–8 | Prep: 40 min | Cooking: 40 min | Level: 1

2 cups (300 g) all-purpose (plain) flour
1 cup (150 g) unsweetened cocoa powder
2 teaspoons baking soda/bicarbonate of soda
1 teaspoon baking powder
½ teaspoon salt
½ cup (125 g) butter, softened
1½ cups (300 g) granulated sugar
2 teaspoons vanilla extract (essence)
2 large eggs, at room temperature
1 cup (250 ml) buttermilk
½ cup (125 ml) strong cold coffee

For the Chocolate Walnut Frosting
4 oz (125 g) semisweet (dark) chocolate,
  coarsely chopped
6 tablespoons butter, cut up
2½ cups (375 g) confectioners' (icing) sugar
1 teaspoon vanilla extract (essence)
1 tablespoon fresh lemon juice
1 cup (100 g) chopped walnuts

Preheat the oven to 350°F (180°C/gas 4). | Butter and flour a 13 x 9-inch (33 x 23-cm) baking pan. | Sift the flour, cocoa, baking soda, baking powder, and salt into a large bowl. | Beat the butter, sugar, and vanilla in a large bowl with an electric mixer at medium speed until creamy. | Add the eggs, one at a time, beating until just blended after each addition. | Gradually beat in the dry ingredients, alternating with the buttermilk and coffee. | Spoon the batter into the prepared pan. | Bake for 30–40 minutes, or until a toothpick inserted into the center comes out clean. | Cool the cake completely in the pan on a rack. | **Chocolate Walnut Frosting:** Melt the chocolate and butter in a double boiler over barely simmering water. Set aside to cool. | Beat in the confectioners' sugar, vanilla, and lemon juice. Add the walnuts. | Spread the top of the cake with the frosting.

double chocolate bundt cake

Serves 8–10 | Prep: 20 min | Cooking: 65 min | Level: 1

2 cups (300 g all-purpose (plain) flour
1/3 cup (50 g) unsweetened cocoa powder
1½ teaspoons baking powder
Pinch of salt
2/3 cup (150 g) butter, softened
4 tablespoons vegetable shortening
2 cups (400 g) granulated sugar
3 large eggs, at room temperature
2/3 cup (150 ml) milk
1 teaspoon vanilla extract (essence)
¾ cup (125 g) semisweet (dark)
    chocolate chips

Preheat the oven to 325°F (170°C/gas 3). | Butter a 10-inch (25-cm) Bundt pan. Dust with cocoa. | Sift the flour, cocoa, baking powder, and salt into a medium bowl. | Beat the butter, shortening, and sugar in a large bowl with an electric mixer at medium speed until creamy. | Add the eggs, one at a time, beating until just blended after each addition. | Gradually beat in the dry ingredients, alternating with the milk and vanilla. | Stir in the chocolate chips. | Spoon the batter into the prepared pan. | Bake for 55–65 minutes, or until a toothpick inserted into the center comes out clean. | Cool in the pan for 10 minutes. Turn out onto a rack to cool completely.

zucchini chocolate bundt cake

Serves 8–10 | Prep: 30 min | Cooking: 65 min | Level: 1

2⅔ cups (400 g) all-purpose (plain) flour
2/3 cup (100 g) unsweetened cocoa powder
2½ teaspoons baking powder
1½ teaspoons baking soda/
    bicarbonate of soda
1 teaspoon ground cinnamon
½ teaspoon salt
¾ cup (180 g) butter, softened
2 cups (400 g) granulated sugar
2 teaspoons vanilla extract (essence)
3 large eggs, at room temperature
1 tablespoon grated orange zest
2 cups (200 g) grated zucchini
1 cup (200 g) chopped walnuts
½ cup (125 ml) milk

For the Orange Vanilla Glaze
1 cup (150 g) confectioners' (icing) sugar
1 tablespoon grated orange zest
2 teaspoons vanilla extract (essence)
1–2 tablespoons fresh orange juice

Preheat the oven to 350°F (180°C/gas 4). | Butter and flour a 10-inch (25-cm) Bundt pan. | Sift the flour, cocoa, baking powder, baking soda, cinnamon, and salt into a large bowl. | Beat the butter, sugar, and vanilla in a large bowl with an electric mixer at medium speed until creamy. | Add the eggs, one at a time, beating until just blended after each addition. | Gradually beat in the dry ingredients, orange zest, zucchini, and walnuts, alternating with the milk. | Spoon the batter into the prepared pan. | Bake for 55–65 minutes, or a toothpick inserted into the center comes out clean. | Cool the cake in the pan for 10 minutes. Turn out onto a rack to cool completely. | **Orange Vanilla Glaze:** Stir the confectioners' sugar, orange zest, and vanilla in a medium bowl. Stir in enough of the orange juice to make a thin glaze. Drizzle the glaze over the warm cake.

basic chocolate cream roll

Serves 8–10 | Prep: 15 min | Cooking: 15 min | Level: 2

8 oz (250 g) semisweet (dark) chocolate,
  coarsely chopped
3 tablespoons water
2 tablespoons strong cold coffee
7 large eggs, separated
¾ cup (150 g) superfine (caster) sugar
Pinch of salt
1⅓ cups (330 ml) heavy (double) cream
⅓ cup (50 g) confectioners' (icing) sugar,
  to dust

Preheat the oven to 350°F (180°C/gas 4). | Butter and flour a 10½ x 15½-inch (26 x 36-cm) jelly-roll pan. Line with parchment paper. | Melt the chocolate with the water and coffee in a double boiler over barely simmering water. Set aside. | Beat the egg yolks and superfine sugar in a large bowl with an electric mixer at high speed until pale and thick. Use a large rubber spatula to fold in the chocolate mixture. | With mixer at high speed, beat the egg whites and salt in a large bowl until stiff peaks form. Fold them into the batter. | Pour the batter into the prepared pan. | Bake for 10–15 minutes, or until a toothpick inserted into the center comes out clean. | Roll up the cake, dusting it with 2 tablespoons confectioners' sugar. | With mixer at high speed, beat the cream in a large bowl until stiff. | Unroll the cake and spread evenly with the cream, leaving a 1-inch (2.5-cm) border. Reroll the cake. | Dust with the remaining confectioners' sugar.

chocolate coffee cream roll

Serves 8–10 | Prep: 15 min | Cooking: 12 min | Level: 2

½ cup (75 g) all-purpose (plain) flour
⅓ cup (50 g) + 2 tablespoons unsweetened
  cocoa powder
½ teaspoon baking powder
5 large eggs, separated
¾ cup (150 g) granulated sugar
2 tablespoons butter, melted
1 teaspoon vanilla extract (essence)
½ teaspoon salt
2 cups (500 ml) Vanilla Pastry Cream
  (see Almond Chocolate Tart, page 52,
  omitting the chocolate), mixed with
  2 tablespoons coffee liqueur

Preheat the oven to 400°F (200°C/gas 6). | Butter and flour a 17 x 12½-inch (43 x 33-cm) jelly-roll pan. Line with parchment paper. | Sift the flour, ⅓ cup (50 g) of cocoa, and baking powder into a large bowl. | Beat the egg yolks, ¼ cup (50 g) of sugar, and butter in a large bowl with an electric mixer at high speed until pale and thick. Add the vanilla. Use a large rubber spatula to fold in the dry ingredients. | With mixer at medium speed, beat the egg whites and salt in a large bowl until frothy. With mixer at high speed, gradually beat in the remaining sugar, beating until stiff, glossy peaks form. Fold them into the batter. | Spoon into the prepared pan. | Bake for 10–12 minutes, or until springy to the touch. | Roll up the cake, dusting it with 2 tablespoons cocoa. | Unroll the cake and spread evenly with the cream, leaving a 1-inch (2.5-cm) border. Reroll the cake.

devil's food cake

Serves 6–8 | Prep: 45 min | Cooking: 40 min | Level: 1

For the Cake
¾ cup (125 g) unsweetened cocoa powder
¾ cup (180 ml) boiling water
2 cups (300 g) all-purpose (plain) flour
2 teaspoons baking powder
½ teaspoon baking soda/bicarbonate of soda
Pinch of salt
¾ cup (180 g) butter, softened
2 cups (400 g) granulated sugar
2 teaspoons vanilla extract (essence)
1 tablespoon chocolate or coffee liqueur
2 large eggs, at room temperature
1 cup (250 ml) buttermilk

For the Frosting
8 oz (200 g) bittersweet (dark) chocolate,
    coarsely chopped
1½ cups (375 g) butter, softened
6 large egg yolks
1 cup (200 g) granulated sugar
½ cup (125 ml) water
2 teaspoons vanilla extract (essence)

Cake: Preheat the oven to 350°F (180°C/gas 4). | Butter two 9-inch (23-cm) round cake pans. Line with waxed paper. Butter the paper. | Stir the cocoa and water in a small bowl until smooth. | Sift the flour, baking powder, baking soda, and salt into a large bowl. | Beat the butter, sugar, vanilla, and liqueur in a large bowl with an electric mixer at medium speed until creamy. | Add the eggs, one at a time, beating until just blended after each addition. | Gradually beat in the dry ingredients, alternating with the buttermilk. | Beat in the cocoa mixture. | Spoon half the batter into each of the prepared pans. | Bake for 30–40 minutes, or until springy to the touch and a toothpick inserted into the centers comes out clean. | Cool the cakes in the pans for 10 minutes. | Turn out onto racks. Carefully remove the paper and let cool completely. | **Frosting**: Melt the chocolate in a double boiler over barely simmering water. Set aside to cool. | With mixer at medium speed, beat the butter in a medium bowl until creamy. | Beat the egg yolks in a large bowl until pale in color. | Place the sugar and water in a medium saucepan over medium-low heat and stir until the sugar has dissolved and the syrup boils. Wash down the sides of the pan with a pastry brush dipped in cold water to prevent sugar crystals from forming. Cook, without stirring, until the syrup reaches 238°F (114°C), or the soft-ball stage. | Remove from the heat. Beat the syrup into the egg yolks in a slow, steady stream. Continue beating until the mixture is cool. Gradually beat in the butter. | Beat in the chocolate and vanilla until creamy. | Place one cake on a serving plate. Spread with one-third of the frosting. Top with the remaining cake. Spread with the remaining frosting.

sacher torte

Serves 6–8 | Prep: 25 min | Cooking: 1 hr | Level: 2

For the Cake
5 oz (150 g) semisweet (dark) chocolate,
    coarsely chopped
6 tablespoons butter, softened
½ cup (100 g) granulated sugar
5 large eggs, separated
⅔ cup (100 g) all-purpose (plain) flour
⅓ cup (110 ml) apricot preserves

For the Frosting
1 tablespoon butter
4 oz (125 g) semisweet (dark) chocolate,
    coarsely chopped
6 tablespoons strong cold coffee
2 cups (300 g) confectioners' (icing) sugar
1 tablespoon vanilla extract (essence)

Cake: Preheat the oven to 325°F (170°C/gas 3). | Set out a 9-inch (23-cm) springform pan. | Melt the chocolate in a double boiler over barely simmering water. Set aside to cool. | Beat the butter and sugar in a large bowl with an electric mixer at medium speed until creamy. | Add the egg yolks, one at a time, beating until just blended after each addition. | Use a large rubber spatula to fold in the chocolate and flour. | With mixer at high speed, beat the egg whites until stiff peaks form. Fold them into the batter. | Spoon the batter into the prepared pan. | Bake for 55–60 minutes, or until a toothpick inserted into the center comes out clean. | Cool the cake in the pan for 20 minutes. Loosen and remove the pan sides and let cool completely. | Split the cake horizontally. Place one layer on a serving plate. Spread with the preserves. Top with the remaining cake. | **Frosting**: Melt the butter and chocolate in a double boiler over barely simmering water. Add the coffee, confectioners' sugar and vanilla. Beat until glossy. | Spread the tops and sides of the cake with the frosting.

Desserts

"And when all these had been eaten ... a cream of chocolate, inspired in the mind, created by the hand of Françoise, would be laid before us, light and fleeting as an 'occasional piece' of music, into which she had poured the whole of her talent. Anyone who refused to partake of it .... would at once have been lowered to the level of the Philistines who, when an artist makes them a present of one of his works, examine its weight and material, whereas what is of value is the creator's intention and his signature. To have left even the tiniest morsel in the dish would have shown as much discourtesy as to rise and leave a concert hall while the 'piece' was still being played, and under the composer's very eyes."
Marcel Proust, Swann's Way (1871–1922)

floating islands with chocolate custard

Serves 8–10 | Prep: 45 min | Cooking: 45 min | Level: 2

For the Chocolate Custard
8 large egg yolks
1 cup (200 g) granulated sugar
2 quarts (2 liters) milk
2 vanilla beans, halved
10 oz (300 g) bittersweet (dark) chocolate,
   finely chopped

For the Floating Islands
16 large egg whites, separated
Pinch of salt
2 cups (400 g) granulated sugar
3 quarts (3 liters) + 1 cup (250 ml)
   cold water

For the Caramel Sauce
2 cups (400 g) granulated sugar
½ cup (125 ml) water

Chocolate Custard: Beat the egg yolks and sugar in a large bowl. Heat the milk with the vanilla in a large saucepan and pour it over the egg mixture. Add the chocolate and mix for 2 minutes until melted. Return the mixture to the saucepan. Cook over low heat, stirring constantly, until the mixture thickens to a pouring consistency. Discard the vanilla. | **Floating Islands:** Beat the egg whites and salt until soft peaks form. Gradually beat in the sugar until stiff peaks form. | Bring the 3 quarts (3 liters) of water to a boil in a large saucepan. Lower the heat to very low and pour in 1 cup (250 ml) cold water to stop it from boiling. | Use 2 dessert spoons to form balls of meringue about the size of golf balls. Drop them into the water to poach for 2 minutes. Use a slotted spoon to turn over and poach for 2 minutes on the other side. Remove from the water and place on a clean cloth. | **Caramel Sauce:** Place the sugar in a heavy-bottomed saucepan with the water and cook until a liquid caramel has formed. | Pour the custard into a large serving dish. Place the meringues on top and drizzle with the caramel.

choc-orange toffee bongo

Serves 6–8 | Prep: 1 hr 20 min | Cooking: 45 min | Level: 3

For the Choux Pastry
6 tablespoons butter, chopped
1 cup (250 ml) water
1 cup (150 g) all-purpose (plain) flour
4 large eggs

For the Orange Chocolate Filling
2 large egg yolks
⅓ cup (70 g) superfine (caster) sugar
1 cup (250 ml) milk
1 tablespoon cornstarch (cornflour)
1 tablespoon all-purpose (plain) flour
2 teaspoons finely grated orange zest
5 oz (150 g) white chocolate, grated
1¼ cups (310 ml) heavy (double) cream

For the Chocolate Toffee
1 cup (200 g) granulated sugar
½ cup (125 ml) water
2½ oz (75 g) bittersweet (plain) chocolate,
   finely chopped

Choux Pastry: Preheat the oven to 400°F (200°C/gas 6). | Butter two baking sheets. | Mix the butter and water in a large saucepan and bring to a boil. Remove from the heat. Add the flour all at once then stir vigorously over low heat until the mixture pulls away from the sides of the pan. | Cool for 5 minutes. | Add the eggs, one at a time, beating after each addition. | Spoon the mixture into a pastry bag fitted with a plain tip. | Pipe mounds of pastry about ¾ inch (2 cm) in diameter onto the prepared baking sheets, spacing 2 inches (5 cm) apart. | Bake for 10 minutes. Lower the oven temperature to 350°F (180°C/gas 4). | Bake for 15 minutes more, or until lightly browned and crisp. Turn off the oven. | Make a small slit in the side of each puff to allow steam to escape. | Return to the cooling oven for about 10 minutes, or until dry and crisp. | Let cool. | **Orange Chocolate Filling:** Beat the egg yolks, sugar, half the milk, cornstarch, and flour in a medium bowl until smooth. Bring the remaining milk and orange zest to a boil in a large saucepan. Gradually stir the milk into the egg mixture until smooth. | Return the mixture to the saucepan, stirring constantly over low heat until the filling thickens. | Remove from the heat and stir in the chocolate. Cool to room temperature. | Beat the cream until soft peaks form and fold it into the filling. | Spoon the filling into a pastry bag fitted with a small plain tip. Pierce the bottom of the puffs and pipe in the filling. | **Chocolate Toffee:** Cook the sugar and water in a small saucepan over low heat, stirring constantly, without boiling, until the sugar has dissolved. Bring to a boil and cook until golden brown. | Place the chocolate in a bowl and slowly stir in the toffee. Carefully dip the tops of the puffs into the chocolate toffee. Arrange the puffs in a pyramid shape on a serving dish.

eggplant with chocolate

Serves 12–14 | Prep: 25 min + 1 hr 15 min to soak the eggplants + 30 min to chill | Cooking: 10 min | Level: 2

8 large, thin slices of eggplant (aubergine
$\frac{2}{3}$ cup (150 g) very fresh Ricotta cheese,
    drained
$\frac{1}{3}$ cup (70 g) granulated sugar
3 oz (90 g) bittersweet (plain) chocolate,
    coarsely grated
$\frac{1}{2}$ cup (50 g) mixed candied fruit, diced
$\frac{1}{2}$ teaspoon vanilla extract (essence)
Four 7-cm (18-cm) rounds of plain
    sponge cake
2 tablespoons Grand Marnier
2 tablespoons sugar
2 tablespoons boiling water

For the Chocolate Sauce
5 oz (150 g) bittersweet (plain) chocolate,
    coarsely chopped
5 tablespoons heavy (double) cream
Candied fruit, to decorate

Fill a large bowl with cold water and add 2 tablespoons of coarse salt. Add the eggplant slices and soak for 1 hour and 15 minutes. | Drain the eggplants and steam them for 10 minutes, or until tender. | Dry with paper towels. | Strain the Ricotta and mix with the sugar in a bowl. | Add the chocolate, candied fruit, and vanilla. | Line 4 individual pudding molds with the slices of eggplant. | Fill the molds with the Ricotta mixture. Cover the top of each mold with a disk of sponge cake. | Mix the Grand Marnier, sugar, and water in a small bowl. Brush the mixture over the sponge cake. | Chill in the refrigerator for 30 minutes. | **Chocolate Sauce:** Melt the chocolate and cream in a double boiler over barely simmering water. | Turn out the molds onto serving dishes and pour the chocolate sauce over the top. Decorate with the candied fruit.

choc and almond toffee dessert

Serves 6–8 | Prep: 30 min | Cooking: 20 min | Level: 2

$\frac{1}{3}$ cup (70 g) superfine (caster) sugar
3 tablespoons water
$\frac{1}{3}$ cup (50 g) finely ground almonds
8 oz (250 g) milk chocolate, melted
8 oz (250 g) semisweet (dark) chocolate,
    melted
4 tablespoons butter, melted
2 tablespoons white rum
1 tablespoon all-purpose (plain) flour
2 teaspoons granulated sugar
2 large eggs, separated

For the Amaretto Cream
1$\frac{1}{4}$ cups (310 ml) heavy (double) cream
$\frac{1}{3}$ cup (50 g) confectioners' (icing) sugar
1 tablespoon amaretto or other almond liqueur

Fresh raspberries, to serve

Preheat the oven to 400°F (200°C/gas 6). | Butter an 8-inch (20-cm) springform pan. Line with waxed paper and butter the paper. | Cook the superfine sugar and water in a small saucepan over low heat, stirring constantly, until the sugar has dissolved. Bring to a boil and boil, without stirring, until golden brown. | Add the almonds and pour the mixture onto a baking sheet. Stand until the toffee has set. | Transfer the toffee to a food processor and process until fine. | Mix the milk and semisweet chocolates, butter, rum, flour, and granulated sugar in a large bowl. | Stir in the egg yolks. | Beat the egg whites in a medium bowl with an electric mixer at high speed until soft peaks form. Fold them into the chocolate mixture. | Spoon the batter into the prepared pan. | Bake for 10 minutes. Sprinkle with one-quarter of the toffee mixture. | Bake for 10 minutes more, or until a toothpick inserted into the center comes out clean. | Cool the cake completely in the pan. | **Amaretto Cream:** Beat the cream and confectioners' sugar in a medium bowl until soft peaks form. | Fold in the remaining toffee and amaretto. | Serve the cake with the amaretto cream and raspberries.

chocolate fondue

Serves 8 | Prep: 15 min | Cooking: 15 min | Level : 2

About 2 lb (1 kg) mixed fresh fruit
  (strawberries, grapes, bananas, apples,
  apricots, peaches, figs, plums, pears, etc.)
2 cups (500 ml) water (optional)
Juice of 1 lemon (optional)
1 lb (500 g) semisweet (dark) chocolate,
  coarsely chopped
1 cup (250 ml) light (single) cream
4 tablespoons butter
4 tablespoons superfine (caster) sugar
1/3 cup (50 g) almonds, toasted and chopped
1/3 cup (50 g) hazelnuts, toasted and chopped
1/3 cup (50 g) shredded (desiccated) coconut

Wash the fruit and dry with care. Cut the larger pieces into bite-sized chunks. | If eating apple, pear, or banana, immerse the fruit in water and lemon juice for a few seconds to prevent the flesh from browning, then dry carefully. | Arrange the fruit in an attractive bowl or serving dish. | Melt the chocolate in a double boiler over barely simmering water. Mix in the cream, then add the butter and superfine sugar and stir thoroughly. | Pour the chocolate mixture into a fondue bowl and keep warm over the flame. | Place bowls filled with the almonds, hazelnuts, and coconut on the table, so that diners can dip their pieces of fruit into them, after having dipped them in the chocolate fondue.

apricot and chocolate bread and butter pudding

Serves 6–8 | Prep: 30 min | Cooking: 60 min | Level: 2

1 loaf day-old white bread, thickly sliced
2 tablespoons butter
1 tablespoon apricot jam
6 large eggs
3/4 cup (150 g) granulated sugar
1 vanilla bean
2 cups (500 ml) light (single) cream
5 oz (150 g) white chocolate, finely chopped
5 oz (150 g) chopped dates

Preheat the oven to 325°F (170°C/gas 3). | Cut the crusts off the bread. Butter the slices and spread them with apricot jam. | Beat the eggs and sugar in a large bowl with an electric mixer at high speed until pale and thick. | Scrape the seeds from the vanilla bean into the cream. Add the pod. | Bring the cream just to a boil in a large saucepan and remove from the heat. | Strain the cream into the egg mixture and whisk lightly. | Butter a deep 9-inch (23-cm) square cake pan and place an even layer of bread on the bottom. Top with a quarter of the chocolate and the dates. | Pour in a quarter of the cream mixture. Repeat the layers until all of the mixture has been used, finishing off with a layer of bread. Press down firmly with a spatula so the bread soaks up the mixture. | Bake for 45-60 minutes, or until golden brown. | Scoop out large servings into bowls and serve with good-quality vanilla ice cream.

cherry fudge crêpes

Serves 4–6 | Prep: 40 min | Cooking: 15 min | Level: 2

For the Crêpes
½ cup (75 g) all-purpose (plain) flour
3 large eggs, lightly beaten
¾ cup (180 ml) milk
1 tablespoon oil
½ cup (160 ml) cherry or raspberry preserves
1 tablespoon cherry brandy

For the Fudge Sauce
½ cup (125 ml) sweetened condensed milk
⅔ cup (150 ml) heavy (double) cream
5 oz (150 g) semisweet (dark) chocolate

For the Cherry Brandy Sauce
4 large egg yolks
⅓ cup (70 g) granulated sugar
1 cup (250 ml) milk
½ cup (125 ml) heavy (double) cream
1 tablespoon cherry brandy
Fresh or canned cherries, to serve

Crêpes: Sift the flour into a large bowl. Make a well in the center and gradually stir in the eggs, milk, and oil until smooth. Cover with plastic wrap (cling film) and refrigerate for 30 minutes. | Wipe a crêpe pan or small frying pan with melted butter. Place the pan over medium heat. Pour 2 tablespoons batter into the crêpe pan, twirling the pan so the the batter covers it thinly. Cook until golden. | Turn over the crêpe and cook the other side until golden. | Repeat with the remaining batter. | Mix the preserves and cherry brandy in a small bowl. Spread over the crêpes and fold into triangles. | **Fudge Sauce:** Mix the condensed milk, cream, and chocolate in a small saucepan. Stir constantly over low heat, without boiling, until smooth. | **Cherry Brandy Sauce:** Beat the egg yolks and sugar in a large bowl until pale and thick. | Bring the milk and cream to a boil in a large saucepan. | Gradually pour the milk into the egg mixture. Return the mixture to the saucepan and cook over low heat until the mixture registers 160°F (71°C) on an instant-read thermometer. Stir in the cherry brandy and set aside to cool. | Serve the crêpes with both sauces and cherries.

rich chocolate pudding

Serves 4–6 | Prep: 40 min + 4 hr to chill | Cooking: 60 min | Level: 2

For the Pudding
6 oz (180 g) bittersweet (dark) chocolate
¾ cup (180 g) butter
1 cup (200 g) granulated sugar
4 large eggs, separated
4 oz (125 g) ladyfingers, crushed
Pinch of salt

For the Chocolate Sauce
5 oz (150 g) bittersweet (dark) chocolate
¾ cup (200 g) granulated sugar
1 cup (250 ml) milk
20–30 raspberries, to decorate

Pudding: Preheat the oven to 350°F (180°C/gas 4). | Butter a 1½-quart (1.5-liter) ovenproof pudding basin. Sprinkle with 3 tablespoons of sugar. | Melt the chocolate in a double boiler over barely simmering water. Set aside to cool. | Beat the butter and remaining sugar in a medium bowl with an electric mixer at high speed until creamy. | Add the egg yolks, one at a time, beating until just blended after each addition. | Gradually beat in the chocolate, followed by the ladyfingers. | Beat the egg whites and salt with an electric mixer at high speed until stiff peaks form. Fold them into the chocolate mixture. | Pour the batter into the prepared basin. Cover with a piece of aluminum foil. Make a small hole in the center of the foil so that steam can escape during cooking. | Place the pudding basin in a large baking dish half-filled with cold water and bake for 50-60 minutes, or until a toothpick inserted into the center comes out clean. | Cool the pudding in the basin for 10 minutes, then carefully turn out onto a serving dish. Let cool to room temperature. Refrigerate for at least 4 hours. | **Chocolate Sauce:** Stir the chocolate, sugar, and milk in a double boiler over barely simmering water until the chocolate is melted. Set aside to cool. | Pour the warm sauce over the pudding, garnish with the raspberries, and serve.

chocolate *vacherin*

Serves 6–8 | Prep: 40 min | Cooking: 60 min | Level: 1

For the Vacherin
5 large egg) whites, at room temperature
1½ cups (300 g) granulated sugar
⅓ cup (50 g) unsweetened cocoa powder
1 teaspoon vanilla extract (essence)

For the Chocolate Ganache
1½ cups (375 ml) heavy (double) cream
1 tablespoon light corn (golden syrup
10 oz (300 g) bittersweet (plain) chocolate,
  coarsely chopped

For the Topping
¾ cup (180 ml) heavy (double) cream
Shavings of bittersweet (dark) chocolate,
  to decorate
Cocoa powder, to dust

Vacherin: Preheat the oven to 275°F (140°C/gas 1). | Line a baking sheet with parchment paper and mark two 9-inch (23-cm) circles on the paper. | Beat the egg whites in a large bowl with an electric mixer at medium speed until frothy. | With mixer at high speed, gradually beat in the sugar, beating until stiff, glossy peaks form. | Use a large rubber spatula to fold in the cocoa and vanilla. | Spoon the mixture into a pastry bag fitted with a ½-inch (1-cm) tip and pipe the mixture into two spiral disks, starting at the center of the drawn circles and filling each circle. | Bake for 50–60 minutes, or until crisp. Turn off the oven and leave the door ajar until the meringues are completely cool. | Carefully remove the paper. | **Chocolate Ganache:** Bring the cream and corn syrup to a boil in a medium saucepan over medium heat. | Remove from heat. | Stir the chocolate into the pan, then set aside for 2 minutes. | Beat until the chocolate has melted and the cream is thick. | About 1 hour before serving, place a meringue layer on a serving plate. Spread with the ganache. Top with the remaining meringue layer. | **Topping:** Beat the cream in a large bowl until stiff. Spread the cream over the top of the cake. Top with the chocolate shavings and dust with the cocoa.

chocolate sponge *dacquoise*

Serves 6–8 | Prep: 45 min + 2 hr to chill | Cooking: 70 min | Level: 2

For the Dacquoise
4 large egg whites, at room temperature
1 cup (200 g) granulated sugar
¾ cup (125 g) finely ground almonds
1 teaspoon almond extract (essence)

For the Chocolate Sponge Cake
¾ cup (125 g) cornstarch (cornflour)
2 tablespoons all-purpose (plain) flour
2 tablespoons unsweetened cocoa powder
1 teaspoon cream of tartar
½ teaspoon baking soda (bicarbonate of soda
4 large eggs, separated
¾ cup (150 g) granulated sugar

For the Chocolate Cream Frosting
6 oz (180 g) bittersweet (dark) chocolate,
  coarsely chopped
1½ cups (375 ml) heavy (double) cream
1 teaspoon vanilla extract (essence)
½ cup (125 ml) dark rum

Dacquoise: Preheat the oven to 300°F (150°C/gas 2). | Butter three 9-inch (23-cm) round cake pans. Line with parchment paper. | Beat the egg whites in a large bowl with an electric mixer at medium speed until frothy. | With mixer at high speed, gradually beat in the sugar, beating until stiff, glossy peaks form. | Use a large rubber spatula to fold the almonds and almond extract into the mixture. | Spoon the batter evenly into the prepared pans. | Bake for 60–70 minutes, or until pale gold and crisp. | Cool the meringues in the pans for 10 minutes. Invert onto racks. Carefully remove the paper and let cool completely. | **Chocolate Sponge Cake:** Preheat the oven to 350°F (180°C/gas 4. | Butter two 9-inch (23-cm) round cake pans. Line with parchment paper. | Sift the cornstarch, flour, cocoa, cream of tartar, and baking soda into a large bowl. | Beat the egg whites in a large bowl with an electric mixer at medium speed until soft peaks form. | Beat in the egg yolks and sugar until pale and thick. Use a large rubber spatula to fold in the dry ingredients. | Bake for 15–20 minutes, or until a toothpick inserted into the center comes out clean. | Cool the cakes in the pans for 15 minutes. Turn out onto racks and carefully remove the paper. Let cool completely. | **Chocolate Cream Frosting:** Melt the chocolate with the cream in a double boiler over barely simmering water. Add the vanilla. Cover and refrigerate until thick and spreadable. | Split the cakes horizontally. Place one layer on a serving plate. Brush with the rum and spread with some of the frosting. Top with a meringue layer and spread with the frosting. Top with a cake layer. Repeat until all the cake, frosting, rum, and meringue have been used, finishing with a layer of frosted cake. | Refrigerate for 2 hours to soften the meringue a little so that the cake can be cut.

nutty chocolate dacquoise

Serves 8–10 | Prep: 30 min | Cooking: 90 min | Level: 2

For the Dacquoise
6 large egg whites, at room temperature
Pinch of salt
1½ cups (300 g) granulated sugar
1½ cups (225 g) finely ground almonds
1 tablespoon cornstarch (cornflour)

For the Filling
8 oz (250 g) bittersweet (dark) chocolate,
    coarsely chopped
1½ cups (375 g) butter, softened
6 large egg yolks, at room temperature
1 cup (200 g) granulated sugar
½ cup (125 ml) water
2 teaspoons vanilla extract (essence)
Toasted hazelnuts, to decorate
Ground hazelnuts, to decorate
Strawberries, to serve

Dacquoise: Preheat the oven to 300°F (150°C/gas 2). | Cut out three 9-inch (23-cm) rounds of parchment paper and place the rounds on baking sheets. | Beat the egg whites and salt in a large bowl with an electric mixer at medium speed until frothy. With mixer at high speed, gradually beat in the sugar, beating until stiff, glossy peaks form. | Use a large rubber spatula to fold in the almonds and cornstarch. | Spoon the meringue into a pastry bag fitted with a ½-inch (1-cm) plain tip. Pipe the meringue in a spiral to fill the rounds, leaving a ½-inch (1-cm) border around the edge. Repeat to fill the other rounds. | Bake for 80–90 minutes, or until crisp. | Cool the meringues for 10 minutes. Transfer onto racks. Carefully remove the paper and let cool completely. | **Filling:** Melt the chocolate in a double boiler over barely simmering water. Set aside to cool. | Beat the butter in a medium bowl with an electric mixer at medium speed until creamy. | With mixer at high speed, beat the egg yolks in a large bowl until pale and thick. | Stir the sugar and water in a saucepan over medium heat until the sugar has dissolved and the syrup boils. Wash down the sides of the pan with a pastry brush dipped in cold water to prevent sugar crystals from forming. Cook, without stirring, until the mixture reaches 238°F (114°C), or the soft-ball stage. | Remove from the heat and slowly beat the syrup into the egg yolks. Continue beating until the mixture is cool. Gradually beat in the butter, followed by the chocolate and vanilla. | Place one meringue layer on a serving plate and spread with one-third of the filling. Top with another meringue layer and spread with one-third of the filling. Place the remaining meringue layer on top. Spread with the remaining filling. | Sprinkle the top of the cake with the toasted hazelnuts. Press the ground hazelnuts around the sides. Serve with strawberries.

chocolate raspberry pudding

Serves 6–8 | Prep: 20 min + 2 hr to chill | Level: 2

2 cups (500 g) raspberries
¼ cup (50 g) superfine (caster) sugar
1 lb (500 g) semisweet (dark) chocolate
½ cup (125 g) butter
2 egg yolks
1 cup (250 ml) heavy (double) cream, whipped
7 oz (200 g) ladyfingers (sponge fingers)
1–2 tablespoons cold espresso coffee
Extra raspberries, to garnish
Cream or crème fraîche, to serve

Mix the raspberries and sugar and set aside. | Melt the chocolate in a double-boiler over barely simmering water. Gradually beat in the butter. s Remove from the heat and let cool slightly before beating in the egg yolks. | Fold in the whipped cream. | Dip each ladyfinger briefly into the coffee and use half of them to line an attractive serving dish. Cover with half the raspberries and sugar. Spoon over half of the chocolate mixture. Repeat, finishing with a chocolate layer. | Refrigerate for at least 2 hours or overnight. | Garnish with the raspberries and serve with whipped cream or crème fraîche.

warm chocolate soufflés with orange liqueur cream

Serves 4 | Prep: 35 min | Cooking: 20 min | Level: 2

For the Chocolate Soufflés
5 oz (150 g) bittersweet (plain) chocolate,
   coarsely chopped
1 cup (250 ml) milk
4 tablespoons butter
1 tablespoon cornstarch (cornflour)
2 tablespoons all-purpose (plain) flour
4 eggs, separated
¼ teaspoon cream of tartar
½ cup (100 g) superfine (caster) sugar

For the Orange Liqueur Cream
1¼ cups (310 ml) heavy (double) cream
1 tablespoon confectioners' (icing) sugar
1 tablespoon Grand Marnier

Chocolate Soufflés: Preheat the oven to 400°F (200°C/gas 6). | Butter four 1-cup (250-ml) soufflé dishes and sprinkle evenly with sugar. | Melt the chocolate with the milk in a large saucepan over low heat, stirring constantly. | Melt the butter in a separate saucepan over low heat. Stir in the cornstarch and flour and cook for 1 minute. | Pour in the chocolate mixture. Cook over medium heat, stirring constantly, until it comes to a boil and begins to thicken. | Remove from the heat and quickly stir in the egg yolks. | Beat the egg whites in a large bowl with an electric mixer at medium speed until soft peaks form. | Add the cream of tartar and sugar and beat at high speed until stiff peaks form. | Use a large rubber spatula to gently fold them into the chocolate mixture in 2 batches. | Pour the mixture intó the prepared dishes. Run your thumb around the top of the dishes to clean off any excess batter. | Bake for about 15 minutes, or until the soufflés have risen slightly over the edge of the dishes. | Prepare the **Orange Liqueur Cream** while the soufflés are baking. Beat the cream, confectioners' sugar, and liqueur in a large bowl until thickened. | Serve the soufflés immediately with the orange liqueur cream.

chocolate soufflé with grand marnier

Serves: 4–6 | Prep: 30 min | Cooking: 10 min | Level: 2

4 oz (125 g) semisweet (dark) chocolate,
   coarsely chopped
4 tablespoons butter
4 large eggs, separated
Grated zest of 1 orange
2 tablespoons Grand Marnier
¼ teaspoon cream of tartar
2 tablespoons confectioners' (icing) sugar,
   to dust

Preheat the oven to 475°F (250°C/gas 8). | Butter and sugar a 1-quart (1-liter) soufflé dish. | Melt the chocolate and butter in a medium saucepan over low heat. | Remove from the heat, whisk in the egg yolks, and pour into a large bowl. | Stir in the orange zest and Grand Marnier. | Beat the egg whites in a large bowl with an electric mixer at medium speed until soft peaks form. | Add the cream of tartar and beat at high speed until stiff peaks form. | Use a large rubber spatula to gently fold them into the chocolate mixture in two batches. | Pour the mixture into the prepared dish. Run your thumb around the top of the dish to clean off any excess batter. | Bake for 5 minutes. | Reduce the oven temperature to 425°F (220°C/gas 7) and bake for 4–5 minutes, or until the soufflé has risen halfway above the top of the dish and is springy to the touch. | Dust with the confectioners' sugar and serve immediately.

chocolate hazelnut steamed pudding

Serves 6–8 | Prep: 35 min | Cooking: 2 hr | Level: 2

½ cup (75 g) all-purpose (plain) flour
½ teaspoon baking powder
4 large eggs
1 cup (200 g) superfine (caster) sugar
½ cup (125 g) butter, chopped
1 cup (150 g) finely ground hazelnuts
8 oz (250 g) semisweet (dark) chocolate, coarsely grated
2 cups (250 g) fine dry bread crumbs

For the Coffee Cream
1¼ cups (310 ml) heavy (double) cream
1 large egg, lightly beaten
2 tablespoons coffee liqueur
1 tablespoon superfine (caster) sugar

Fresh apricots, to serve
Coarsely chopped walnuts, to serve

Butter a 1½-quart (1.5-liter) pudding basin or heatproof bowl. | Sift the flour and baking powder into a large bowl. | Beat the eggs and sugar in a large bowl with an electric mixer at high speed until pale and fluffy. | Gradually beat in the butter until well blended. | Use a large rubber spatula to fold in the hazelnuts, chocolate, bread crumbs, and the dry ingredients. | Pour the batter into the prepared basin. Cover with waxed paper and a layer of aluminum foil. Secure with kitchen string or cover with the lid. | Place the basin in a large saucepan and pour in enough boiling water to reach halfway up the sides. | Cover and simmer for about 2 hours or until firm. | **Coffee Cream:** Mix the cream, egg, coffee liqueur, and sugar in a small saucepan over low heat. Stir constantly until the cream thickens slightly. | Serve the pudding with the coffee cream and sliced apricots and walnuts.

chocolate and lemon cheesecake

Serves 6–8 | Prep: 30 min + 6 hr 30 min to chill | Cooking: 55 min | Level: 1

For the Chocolate Crumb Base
1½ cups (180 g) chocolate wafer crumbs
8 tablespoons butter, melted
1 teaspoon pumpkin pie spice

For the Filling
7 oz (200 g) white chocolate, coarsely chopped
½ cup (125 ml) heavy (double) cream
2 cups (500 ml) cream cheese, softened
¾ cup (150 g) granulated sugar
3 large eggs, at room temperature
2 tablespoons grated lemon zest
4 tablespoons fresh lemon juice

For the Lemon Glaze
2 cups (300 g) confectioners' (icing) sugar
4 tablespoons fresh lemon juice
1½ teaspoons grated lemon zest

Butter a 9-inch (23-cm) springform pan. | **Chocolate Crumb Base:** Mix the crumbs, butter, and pumpkin pie spice in a medium bowl. Press into the bottom and partway up the sides of the prepared pan. Refrigerate for 30 minutes. | Preheat the oven to 350°F (180°C/gas 4). | **Filling:** Melt the chocolate and cream in a double boiler over barely simmering water. Set aside to cool. | Beat the cream cheese and sugar in a large bowl with an electric mixer at low speed until creamy. | Add the eggs, one at a time, beating until just blended after each addition. | Beat in the lemon zest and juice and the chocolate mixture. | Spoon the filling into the crumb base. | Bake for 45–55 minutes, or until set. | Cool the cheesecake in the oven with the door ajar for 30 minutes. | Remove from the oven and cool completely on a rack. | **Lemon Glaze:** Sift the confectioners' sugar into a small bowl. Beat in the lemon juice and zest until smooth and spreadable. | Spread the glaze over the cheesecake. | Refrigerate for 6 hours. Loosen and remove the pan sides to serve.

mocha cheesecake

Serves 8–10 | Prep: 30 min + 6 hr to chill | Cooking: 65 min | Level: 1

For the Chocolate Crumb Base

1¾ cups (220 g) chocolate wafer crumbs

4 tablespoons butter, melted

2 tablespoons granulated sugar

1 teaspoon ground cinnamon

For the Filling

8 oz (250 g) semisweet (dark) chocolate, coarsely chopped

2 tablespoons heavy (double) cream

3 cups (750 g) cream cheese, softened

1 cup (200 g) granulated sugar

3 large eggs, at room temperature

1 cup (250 ml) sour cream

4 tablespoons coffee liqueur

2 teaspoons freeze-dried coffee granules, dissolved in 4 tablespoons hot water

2 teaspoons vanilla extract (essence)

For the Topping

1 cup (250 ml) heavy (double) cream

2 tablespoons confectioners' (icing) sugar

2 tablespoons coffee liqueur

2 oz (60 g) semisweet (dark) chocolate, coarsely grated

Preheat the oven to 350°F (180°C/gas 4). | Butter a 10-inch (25-cm) springform pan. | **Chocolate Crumb Base:** Mix the crumbs, butter, sugar, and cinnamon in a medium bowl. | Press into the bottom and partway up the sides of the prepared pan. | **Filling:** Melt the chocolate with the cream in a double boiler over barely simmering water. Set aside to cool. | Beat the cream cheese and sugar in a large bowl with an electric mixer at high speed until creamy. | Add the eggs, one at a time, beating until just blended after each addition. | Gradually beat in the chocolate mixture, sour cream, coffee liqueur, coffee mixture, and vanilla. | Spoon the filling into the crumb base. | Bake for 55–65 minutes, or until set. | Cool the cheesecake in the oven with the door ajar for 30 minutes. | Remove from the oven and cool completely on a rack. | Refrigerate for 6 hours. | **Topping:** Beat the cream, confectioners' sugar, and coffee liqueur in a medium bowl until stiff. | Loosen and remove the pan sides. Spread with the topping and sprinkle with the chocolate.

 fudge brownie cheesecake

Serves 8–10 | Prep: 1 hr + 6 hr to chill | Cooking: 1 hr 40 min | Level: 2

For the Brownie

4 oz (125 g) bittersweet (plain) chocolate, coarsely chopped

½ cup (125 g) cold butter, cut up

1½ cups (300 g) granulated sugar

2 large eggs, at room temperature

1 cup (150 g) all-purpose (plain) flour

Pinch of salt

4 tablespoons milk

1 teaspoon vanilla extract (essence)

½ cup (50 g) chopped walnuts

For the Filling

3 cups (750g) cream cheese, softened

½ cup (100 g) granulated sugar

2 teaspoons vanilla extract (essence)

½ cup (125 ml) sour cream

4 large eggs, at room temperature

Preheat the oven to 350°F (180°C/gas 4). | Butter and flour a 10-inch (25-cm) springform pan. | **Brownie:** Melt the chocolate and butter in a double boiler over barely simmering water. Set aside to cool for 15 minutes. | Transfer to a bowl. Beat in the sugar with an electric mixer at medium speed. | Add the eggs, one at a time, beating until just blended after each addition. | Gradually beat in the flour and salt, alternating with the milk and vanilla extract. Stir in the walnuts. | Spoon the batter into the prepared pan. | Bake for 35–40 minutes, or until set. | Cool completely in the pan on a rack. | **Filling:** Beat the cream cheese, sugar, and vanilla in a large bowl until smooth. Add the sour cream and eggs. | Spoon the filling over the brownie. | Bake for 55–60 minutes, or until set. | Cool the cheesecake in the pan on a rack. | Refrigerate for 6 hours. Loosen and remove the pan sides to serve.

peanut chocolate cheesecake

Serves 8–10 | Prep: 35 min + 6 hr to chill | Cooking: 65 min | Level: 1

For the Peanut Crumb Base
1½ cups (180 g) graham cracker crumbs
¼ cup (50 g) granulated sugar
3 tablespoons creamy peanut butter
1 tablespoon butter, melted
1 teaspoon ground cinnamon

For the Filling
8 oz (250 g) semisweet (dark) chocolate, coarsely chopped
3 cups (750 g) cream cheese, softened
1 cup (200 g) granulated sugar
5 large eggs, at room temperature
2 tablespoons all-purpose (plain) flour
4 tablespoons milk
⅔ cup (150 g) creamy peanut butter
1 teaspoon vanilla extract (essence)

Butter a 10-inch (25-cm) springform pan. | **Peanut Crumb Base:** Mix the crumbs, sugar, peanut butter, butter, and cinnamon in a medium bowl. | Press into the bottom and partway up the sides of the prepared pan. | Refrigerate for 30 minutes. | Preheat the oven to 375°F (190°C/gas 5). | **Filling:** Melt the chocolate in a double boiler over barely simmering water. Set aside to cool. | Beat the cream cheese and sugar in a large bowl with electric mixer at medium speed until creamy. | Add the eggs, one at a time, beating until just blended after each addition. | Gradually beat in the flour, alternating with the milk. | Place one-third of the batter in a small bowl and add the peanut butter. Place another one-third of the batter in small bowl and add the chocolate. Stir the vanilla into the remaining filling. | Spoon alternate dollops of the three different fillings into the crust . Use a knife to swirl them attractively. | Bake for 55-65 minutes, or until set. | Cool the cheesecake in the oven with the door ajar for 30 minutes. | Remove from the oven and cool completely on a rack. | Refrigerate for 6 hours. Loosen and remove the pan sides to serve.

orange chocolate cheesecake

Serves 6–8 | Prep: 30 min + 6 hr 30 min to chill | Cooking: 70 min | Level: 2

For the Chocolate Crumb Base
1¾ cups (220 g) graham cracker crumbs
¼ cups (50 g) granulated sugar
1 tablespoon unsweetened cocoa powder
1 teaspoon ground cinnamon
4 tablespoons butter, melted

For the Filling
8 oz (250 g) bittersweet (dark) chocolate, coarsely chopped
2 cups (500 g) cream cheese, softened
½ cup (125 ml) sour cream
1 cup (200 g) granulated sugar
1 tablespoon grated orange zest
5 large eggs, at room temperature

For the Topping
1 cup (250 ml) heavy (double) cream
2 tablespoons grated orange zest, to decorate

Preheat the oven to 350°F (180°C/gas 4). | Butter a 9-inch (23-cm) springform pan. | **Chocolate Crumb Base:** Mix the crumbs, sugar, cocoa, cinnamon, and butter in a medium bowl. | Press into the bottom and partway up the sides of the prepared pan. | Refrigerate for 30 minutes. | **Filling:** Melt the chocolate in a double boiler over barely simmering water. | Beat the cream cheese in a large bowl with an electric mixer at high speed until creamy. | Beat in the sour cream, sugar, orange zest, and the melted chocolate. | Add the eggs, one at a time, beating until just blended after each addition. | Spoon the filling into the crumb base. | Bake for 60-70 minutes, or until set. | Cool the cheesecake in the oven with the door ajar for 30 minutes. | Remove from the oven and cool completely on a rack. | Refrigerate for 6 hours. Loosen and remove the pan sides. Transfer to a serving plate. | **Topping:** Beat the cream in a medium bowl until stiff. Spread the cream on top of the cheesecake and sprinkle with the orange zest.

chocolate liqueur suicide cake

Serves 8–10 | Prep: 45 min + 15 min to freeze + 6 hr to chill | Cooking: 70 min | Level: 2

For the Chocolate Crumb Base

1½ cups (180 g) graham cracker crumbs
¾ cup (75 g) chopped almonds or hazelnuts
7 tablespoons butter, melted
¼ cup (50 g) granulated sugar
6 oz (180 g) semisweet (dark) chocolate, coarsely chopped

For the Filling

1 lb (500 g) bittersweet (plain) chocolate, coarsely chopped
1½ cups (375 ml) heavy (double) cream
2 tablespoons unsweetened cocoa powder
¾ cup (180 ml) Irish cream liqueur
2 lb (1 kg) cream cheese, softened
1 cup (200 g) granulated sugar
1 teaspoon vanilla extract (essence)
4 large eggs, at room temperature

Preheat the oven to 350°F (180°C/gas 4). | Butter a 10-inch (25-cm) springform pan. | **Chocolate Crumb Base**: Mix the crumbs, nuts, butter, and sugar in a medium bowl. | Press into the bottom and partway up the sides of the prepared pan. | Bake for 8–10 minutes, or until lightly browned. | Cool completely in the pan on a rack. | Melt the semisweet chocolate in a double boiler over barely simmering water. Set aside to cool. | Pour the chocolate over the crumb base. Freeze for 15 minutes. | **Filling**: Melt the chocolate in a double boiler over barely simmering water. Set aside to cool. | Warm ½ cup (125 ml) of cream in a saucepan over low heat. Add the cocoa and cook, stirring constantly, until the cream begins to thicken. Remove from the heat. Add the liqueur and remaining cream and set aside to cool. | Beat the cream cheese, sugar, and vanilla in a large bowl with an electric mixer at medium speed until smooth. | Add the eggs, one at a time, beating until just blended after each addition. | With mixer at low speed, beat in the cocoa mixture and chocolate. | Spoon the filling into the crust. | Bake for 50–60 minutes, or until set. | Cool the cheesecake in the oven with the door ajar for 30 minutes. | Remove from the oven and cool completely on a rack. | Refrigerate for 6 hours. Loosen and remove the pan sides to serve.

chocolate chip amaretto cake

Serves 8–10 | Prep: 2 min + 6 hr to chill | Cooking: 60 min | Level: 1

For the Amaretti Crumb Base

2 cups (250 g) crushed amaretti cookies
½ cup (50 g) finely chopped almonds
½ cup (125 g) butter, melted

For the Filling

3 cups (750 g) cream cheese, softened
1 cup (200 g) granulated sugar
2 tablespoons cornstarch (cornflour)
3 large eggs, at room temperature
3 tablespoons amaretto
1 tablespoon vanilla extract (essence)
¾ cup (135 g) semisweet chocolate chips

Preheat the oven to 400°F (200°C/gas 6). | Butter a 10-inch (25-cm) springform pan. | **Amaretti Crumb Base**: Mix the crumbs, almonds, and butter in a medium bowl. | Press into the bottom and partway up the sides of the prepared pan. | Bake for 8–10 minutes, or until lightly browned. | Cool completely in the pan on a rack. | **Filling**: Beat the cream cheese, sugar, and cornstarch in a large bowl with an electric mixer at medium speed until smooth. | Add the eggs, one at a time, beating until just blended after each addition. | Beat in the amaretto and vanilla. Stir in the chocolate chips. | Spoon the filling into the crumb base. | Bake for 50–60 minutes, or until set. | Cool the cheesecake in the oven with the door ajar for 30 minutes. | Remove from the oven and cool completely on a rack. | Refrigerate for 6 hours. Loosen and remove the pan sides to serve.

tiramisù cheesecake

Serves 6–8 | Prep: 20 min + 6 hr to chill | Cooking: 40 min | Level: 1

For the Ladyfinger Base
12 ladyfingers (sponge fingers), cut in half lengthwise
6 tablespoons strong cold coffee
4 tablespoons kirsch

For the Filling
2 cups (500 g) cream cheese, softened
½ cup (100 g) granulated sugar
2 teaspoons vanilla extract (essence)
2 large eggs, at room temperature
1 cup (250 ml) heavy (double) cream
2 oz (60 g) semisweet (dark) chocolate, grated

Preheat the oven to 350°F (180°C/gas 4). | Butter a 9-inch (23-cm) springform pan. | **Ladyfinger Base:** Arrange the ladyfingers in the prepared pan, fitting them together tightly, and using small pieces to fill in any gaps. Cut the remaining ladyfingers in half crosswise. Arrange with the flat sides against the pan sides. | Mix the coffee and kirsch in a small bowl and drizzle over the ladyfingers. | **Filling:** Beat the cream cheese, sugar, and vanilla in a large bowl with an electric mixer at medium speed until creamy. | Add the eggs, one at a time, beating until just blended after each addition. | Spoon the cheese mixture into the pan. | Bake for 35–40 minutes, or until set. | Cool the cheesecake in the oven with the door ajar for 30 minutes. | Remove from the oven and cool completely on a rack. | Refrigerate for 6 hours. | Beat the cream in a medium bowl until stiff. Loosen and remove the pan sides. | Spread the cream over the top of the cheesecake and sprinkle with the chocolate.

chocolate cherry cheesecake

Serves 6–8 | Prep: 25 min + 6 hr to chill | Cooking: 55 min | Level: 1

For the Crumb Base
1½ cups (180 g) graham cracker crumbs
4 tablespoons butter, melted
2 tablespoons brown sugar
½ teaspoon ground nutmeg

For the Filling
4 oz (125 g) semisweet (dark) chocolate, coarsely chopped
2 cups (500 g) cream cheese, softened
¾ cup (150 g) granulated sugar
½ teaspoon vanilla extract (essence)
2 large eggs, at room temperature

For the Cherry Topping
1 cup (250 ml) heavy (double) cream
2 tablespoons confectioners' (icing) sugar
½ teaspoon vanilla extract (essence)
1½ cups (375 ml) cherry pie filling

Preheat the oven to 350°F (180°C/gas 4). | Butter a 9-inch (23-cm) springform pan. | **Crumb Base:** Mix the crumbs, butter, brown sugar, and nutmeg in a medium bowl. | Press into the bottom and partway up the sides of the prepared pan. | Bake for 8–10 minutes, or until lightly browned. | Cool completely in the pan on a rack. | **Filling:** Melt the chocolate in a double boiler over barely simmering water. Set aside to cool. | Beat the cream cheese, sugar, and vanilla in a large bowl with an electric mixer at medium speed until creamy. | Add the eggs, one at a time, beating until just blended after each addition. | Beat in the chocolate. | Spoon the filling into the crumb base. | Bake for 35–45 minutes, or until set. | Cool the cheesecake in the oven with the door ajar for 30 minutes. | Remove from the oven and cool completely on a rack. | Refrigerate for 6 hours. | **Cherry Topping:** Beat the cream, confectioners' sugar, and vanilla in a medium bowl until stiff. | Loosen and remove the pan sides. Spread with the cherry pie filling and decorate with the cream.

chocolate mousse

Serves 4–6 | Prep: 20 min + 4 hr to chill | Cooking: 10 min | Level: 2

12 oz (300 g) bittersweet (plain) chocolate
½ cup (125 ml) milk
6 large eggs, separated
½ cup (75 g) confectioners' (icing) sugar
¾ cup (180 ml) heavy (double) cream
¼ teaspoon cream of tartar
2 tablespoons granulated sugar

Melt the chocolate with the milk in a double boiler over barely simmering water. | Beat the egg yolks and confectioners' sugar in a double boiler until well blended. Stir in the chocolate mixture. Cook over low heat, stirring constantly with a wooden spoon, until the mixture lightly coats a metal spoon or registers 160°F (71°C) on an instant-read thermometer. Immediately plunge the pan into a bowl of ice water and stir until the egg mixture has cooled. | Beat the cream in a large bowl with an electric mixer at high speed until stiff. Fold it into the chocolate mixture. | Stir the egg whites, cream of tartar, and sugar in a double boiler until blended. Cook over low heat, beating constantly with an electric mixer at low speed until the whites register 160°F (71°C) on an instant-read thermometer. Beat at high speed until stiff peaks form. | Fold them into the chocolate mixture. | Refrigerate for 4 hours.

chocolate walnut ice cream

Serves 4–6 | Prep: 25 min + 12 hr to freeze | Cooking: 5 min | Level: 2

5 oz (150 g) semisweet (dark) chocolate,
   coarsely chopped
1¾ cups (430 ml) heavy (double) cream
2 teaspoons instant coffee granules
5 large egg yolks
⅓ cup (70 g) superfine (caster) sugar
1 tablespoon dark rum
1 cup (100 g) chopped walnuts
3½ oz (100 g) semisweet (dark)
   chocolate chips

Melt the chocolate with the cream and coffee in a medium saucepan over low heat, stirring constantly. Remove from the heat. Beat the egg yolks and sugar in a double boiler until blended. Gradually beat in the hot cream mixture. Cook over low heat, stirring constantly with a wooden spoon, until the mixture lightly coats a metal spoon or registers 160°F (71°C) on an instant-read thermometer. Immediately plunge the pan into a bowl of ice water and stir until the egg mixture has cooled. | Stir in the rum, pour into a large bowl, and cover with plastic wrap (cling film). | Cool to room temperature and pour into a 9 x 5-inch (23 x 13-cm) loaf pan. Cover with aluminum foil and freeze for 2 hours, or until partly set. | Remove from the pan and beat until smooth. Stir in the nuts and chocolate chips. Return to the pan, cover with foil, and freeze until set.

gelato alla crema

Serves 4–6 | Prep: 30 min + 9 hr to freeze (without ice-cream machine) | Cooking: 15 min | Level: 2

2 cups (500 ml) milk
1 cup (250 ml) heavy (double) cream
4 large egg yolks
1 cup (200 g) granulated sugar

Use this recipe as the basis of a delicious chocolate ice cream. It complements most of the cakes and desserts in this book, underlining the sumptuous taste of chocolate without detracting from it.

Bring the milk and cream to a boil in a saucepan. | Remove from the heat and cool slightly. Beat the egg yolks and sugar in a double boiler until well blended. | Gradually pour in the warm milk mixture. | Cook over low heat, stirring constantly with a wooden spoon, until the mixture lightly coats a metal spoon or registers 160°F (71°C) on an instant-read thermometer. Immediately plunge the pan into a bowl of ice water and stir until the egg mixture has cooled. | If you have an ice-cream machine, pour the mixture into it and follow the instructions on your machine. | If you don't have an ice-cream machine, pour the mixture into a large bowl and freeze for 9 hours, stirring well every 3 hours.

hazelnut ice-cream

Serves 4–6 | Prep: 30 min + 9 hr to freeze (without ice-cream machine) | Cooking: 15 min | Level: 2

1 quantity Gelato alla crema (see above)
2 tablespoons unsweetened cocoa powder
4 tablespoons finely ground hazelnuts
½ cup (125 ml) heavy (double) cream
4 tablespoons chocolate chips

Prepare the ice-cream, dissolving the cocoa powder and hazelnuts in the hot milk and cream mixture. | Serve in individual ice-cream dishes. Whip the cream until stiff and use it to decorate each serving. Sprinkle with the chocolate chips and serve.

raspberry chocolate ice cream

Serves 4–6 | Prep: 30 min + 9 hr to freeze (without ice-cream machine) | Cooking: 15 min | Level: 2

1 quantity Gelato alla crema
  (see recipe, page 131)
4 tablespoons unsweetened cocoa powder
1 lb (500 g) raspberries
Fresh mint leaves, to decorate

Prepare the ice-cream, dissolving the cocoa powder in the hot milk and cream mixture. | When the ice-cream is ready, serve in individual ice-cream dishes. Garnish each serving with the raspberries and fresh mint leaves.

cognac sorbet

Serves 4 | Prep: 25 min + 4 hr to freeze | Cooking: 5 min | Level: 1

1 quart (1 liter) water
2½ cups (500 g) granulated sugar
⅔ cup (100 g) unsweetened cocoa powder
4 tablespoons Cognac
¾ cup (180 ml) crème fraîche or sour cream
⅔ cup (100 g) confectioners' (icing) sugar

Bring 2 cups (500 ml) of water and sugar to a boil in a large saucepan. Boil for 2 minutes. | Pour in the remaining water and cocoa and mix well. | Add 2 tablespoons of Cognac. | Pour the mixture into in a freezerproof container and freeze until mushy. | Mash lightly and refreeze. | Beat the crème fraîche, confectioners' sugar, and the remaining Cognac in a small bowl until creamy. | Serve the sorbet with the crème fraîche mixture.

chocolate bombe

Serves 8–10 | Prep: 25 min + 12 hr to freeze the bombe | Cooking: 3 min | Level: 1

4 oz (125 g) semisweet (dark) chocolate,
  melted
4 oz (125 g) milk chocolate, melted
4 oz (125 g) white chocolate, melted
7 tablespoons butter, melted
½ cup (90 g) golden raisins (sultanas
4 tablespoons amaretto
2 quarts (2 liters) chocolate ice cream
1 cup (180 g) white chocolate chips

Line a 2½-quart (2.5-liter) bowl with plastic wrap (cling film). | Place each of the 3 types of chocolate in three small bowls. Divide butter evenly between the bowls and stir until smooth. Drop spoonfuls of each of the 3 mixtures into the lined bowl, smoothing the surface with a spatula to form a shell. Freeze until set. | Cook the golden raisins in the liqueur in a small saucepan over medium heat. Simmer for 3 minutes, or until most of the liqueur has been absorbed. Set aside to cool. | Soften the ice cream at room temperature. Stir in the raisin mixture and chocolate chips. Spoon the ice cream into the frozen chocolate shell. | Freeze overnight. | Turn onto a serving plate and carefully peel away the plastic wrap.

hot chocolate almond delights

Serves 6 | Prep: 30 min | Cooking: 30 min | Level: 1

For the Puddings
1 cup (150 g) all-purpose (plain) flour
1 teaspoon baking powder
3 tablespoons unsweetened cocoa powder,
$\frac{1}{8}$ teaspoon salt
$\frac{1}{2}$ cup (75 g) finely ground almonds
$\frac{1}{2}$ cup (100 g) superfine (caster) sugar
$\frac{1}{2}$ cup (125 ml) milk
$3\frac{1}{2}$ oz (100 g) bittersweet (dark) chocolate,
   melted
$\frac{1}{3}$ cup (80 g) butter, melted

For the Topping
$\frac{1}{2}$ cup (100 g) firmly packed dark brown sugar
4 tablespoons unsweetened cocoa powder
$1\frac{1}{2}$ cups (375 ml) boiling water
2 tablespoons unsweetened cocoa powder,
   to dust

For the Almond Cream
$1\frac{1}{2}$ cups (310 ml) heavy (double) cream
2 tablespoons confectioners' (icing) sugar
1 tablespoon amaretto liqueur

Preheat the oven to 350°F (180°C/gas 4). | Butter six 1-cup (250-ml) soufflé dishes. | **Puddings**: Sift the flour, baking powder, cocoa and salt into a medium bowl. Stir in almonds, sugar, milk, chocolate, and butter. | Divide the mixture evenly among the prepared dishes. Stand the dishes on a baking sheet. | Topping: Mix the brown sugar and cocoa in a small bowl and sprinkle evenly over each dessert. Pour the boiling water evenly over the brown sugar and cocoa. | Bake for about 30 minutes, or until set. Let cool to warm. | Dust with the cocoa. | Almond Cream: Beat cream and sugar in a small bowl until thick. Fold in the amaretto. Spoon a little cream onto each dessert and serve.

chocolate sponge pudding

Serves 2–4 | Prep: 20 min | Cooking: 50 min | Level: 2

1 tablespoon butter
2 tablespoons self-rising flour
2 tablespoon unsweetened cocoa powder
$\frac{3}{4}$ cup (150 g) superfine (caster) sugar
1 teaspoon finely grated orange zest
4 tablespoons freshly squeezed orange juice
2 eggs, separated
1 cup (250 ml) milk
$3\frac{1}{2}$ oz (100 g) semisweet (dark) chocolate,
   coarsely chopped
$\frac{1}{2}$ cup (125 ml) heavy (double) cream,
   whipped

Preheat the oven to 350°F (180°C/gas 4). | Melt the butter in a bowl. Sift in the flour and cocoa, add the sugar and then stir in the orange zest and juice. Mix thoroughly. | Beat the egg whites until stiff peaks form. | Beat the yolks and milk together and stir into the chocolate mixture. | Fold the whites carefully but thoroughly into the mixture. | Pour into a deep, medium-sized baking dish and sprinkle with the chocolate. Place in a larger ovenproof container half filled with cold water and bake for 60 minutes, or until set. | Serve warm with the whipped cream.

orange white chocolate mousse

Serves 4 | Prep: 30 min + 4 hr to chill || Level: 2

4 oz (125 g) white chocolate, coarsely
   chopped
4 large egg yolks
3 tablespoons superfine (caster) sugar
2 teaspoons gelatin dissolved in
   2 tablespoons warm water
2 tablespoons Cointreau
1 cup (250 ml) heavy (double) cream

Almond tuile cookies, to serve

Melt the chocolate in a double boiler over barely simmering water. | Beat the egg yolks and sugar until pale and creamy. | Fold in the melted chocolate, followed by the dissolved gelatin. Stir in the Cointreau. Let cool. | Whip the cream until stiff then fold into the cooled chocolate mixture. | Pour into a small, deep serving bowl. | Refrigerate for 4 hours before serving. | Serve with the almond tuile cookies.

chocolate orange crème brulée

Serves 6 | Prep: 30 min + 4 hr to chill | Cooking: 30 min
| Level: 2

2 large sweet oranges, peeled and chopped
1¼ cups (310 ml) heavy (double) cream
1¼ cups (310 ml) crème fraîche
1 vanilla bean
4 oz (125 g) bittersweet (dark) chocolate,
   coarsely chopped
4 large egg yolks
1 tablespoon cointreau

For the Topping
6 tablespoons demerrara sugar

Choose sweet, deep-red blood oranges for this fabulous dessert.

Divide the chopped orange among 6 ramekins or other flameproof dishes and set on a baking sheet. | Mix the cream, crème fraîche, and vanilla bean in the top of a double boiler over barely simmering water. Heat the mixture for 10 minutes, then remove the vanilla bean. | Gradually stir in the chocolate until melted and smooth. Remove the top pan, leaving the pan of water over the heat. | Beat the egg yolks and cointreau in another heatproof bowl until well mixed. Gradually pour in the chocolate mixture, beating constantly. | Place the bowl over the pan of simmering water and stir constantly until the chocolate custard is thick enough to coat the back of a spoon. Remove from the heat. Spoon the chocolate over the oranges. Let cool to room temperature | Refrigerate for 4 hours. | Topping: Sprinkle each custard with 1 tablespoon of the demerrara sugar and melt with a torch or under the broiler. Serve immediately.

kahlua mousse

Serves 6 | Prep: 20 min + 4 hr to chill | Cooking: 10 min | Level: 1

1 lb (500 g) bittersweet (dark) chocolate,
    coarsely chopped
1 (3 cup (90 g) butter, cut up
1 (4 cup (60 g) confectioners' (icing) sugar
3 large eggs, separated
4 tablespoons Kahlua liqueur
1 teaspoon freeze-dried coffee granules
2 cups (500 ml) heavy (double) cream

Melt the chocolate with the butter in the top of a double boiler over simmering water. | Place the confectioners' sugar, egg yolks, Kahlua, and coffee in a large bowl. | Stir in the chocolate mixture. | Whip the cream until stiff then fold it into the Kahlua-chocolate mixture. | Beat the egg whites until just stiff. Fold them into the mixture. | Spoon the mixture into a deep serving dish. | Chill in the refrigerator for at least 4 hours before serving.

mascarpone chocolate cream

Serves 6 | Prep: 30 min + 2 hr to chill | Level: 1

2 large egg yolks
½ cup (100 g) granulated sugar
10 oz/300 g) Mascarpone cheese
1 tablespoon dry Marsala wine
4 oz (125 g) bittersweet (dark) chocolate,
    coarsely chopped
3 tablespoons milk
6 small meringues

Beat the egg yolks and sugar until very pale and creamy. | Mix in the Mascarpone gently and flavor with the Marsala. | Melt the chocolate with the milk in a double boiler over barely simmering water. Set aside to cool. | Mix the chocolate-milk mixture into half of the Mascarpone mixture. | Crumble the meringues into the bottom of six ice-cream dishes and spoon in the Mascarpone and chocolate mixtures. | Blend the surfaces of the two mixtures with a knife to give a marbled effect, or leave them separate, as preferred. | Chill in the refrigerator for at least 2 hours before serving.

chocolate zabaglione

Serves 4 | Prep: 20 min | Cooking: 15 min | Level: 1

5 large egg yolks
½ cup (100 g) superfine (caster) sugar
½ cup (125 ml) dry marsala
2 tablespoons unsweetened cocoa powder
4 tablespoons grated bittersweet (dark)
   chocolate, to serve
Fresh raspberries, to serve

Place the egg yolks and sugar in a double boiler (or in a heatproof bowl). Beat with a whisk until pale and creamy. | Place the marsala in a small bowl, add the cocoa, and stir until smooth. | Beat the marsala mixture into the egg mixture, then place over barely simmering water. | Cook, beating constantly until the mixture is thick and creamy, 10–15 minutes. Make sure the mixture does not come to a boil during cooking, or it will curdle. | Let the zabaglione cool slightly. Spoon into 4 serving glasses. | Let cool to room temperature, then refrigerate. | Garnish with the grated chocolate and raspberries just before serving.

jaffa mousse

Serves 6 | Prep: 15 min + 3 hr to chill | Cooking: 10 min |
Level: 1

10 oz (300 g) bittersweet (dark) chocolate
1 cup (250 g) butter
4 tablespoons Grand Marnier liqueur
2 cups (500 ml) heavy (double) cream
8 large eggs, separated
½ cup (100 g) granulated sugar

Place the chocolate, butter, and Grand Marnier in the top of a double boiler over simmering water until melted. Set aside to cool. | Beat the egg yolks and sugar until the mixture fall in ribbons. This will take about 10 minutes. | In a large bowl, combine the chocolate sauce with the egg mixture. Beat with a wire whisk until thick. | In another large bowl, beat the egg whites until stiff peaks form. Fold the egg whites into the chocolate sauce until just combined. | Beat the cream until stiff and fold it into the chocolate mixture. | Spoon into one large or six individual serving dishes and refrigerate for at least 3 hours before serving.

Candy

"Look, there's no metaphysics on earth like chocolates."
Fernando Pessoa (1888-1935)

dusky truffles

Makes about 30 truffles | Prep: 20 min + 4 hr to chill |
Cooking: 5 min | Level: 1

8 oz (250 g) bittersweet (dark) chocolate
1 cup (250 ml) heavy (double) cream
2 tablespoons dark rum
½ cup (75 g) unsweetened cocoa powder,
   to dust
Shredded (desiccated) coconut, to decorate
Finely chopped almonds, to decorate

Place the chocolate in a large bowl. | Heat the cream in a saucepan and pour it over the chocolate. Stir until the chocolate has melted and the mixture is smooth and well blended. | Set aside to cool. | Refrigerate for 3–4 hours, or until the mixture is thick. | Sift the cocoa into a dessert plate. Dust your hands with cocoa. Shape the mixture into truffles about the size of a large marble. | Roll one-third of the truffles in the coconut, one-third in the almonds, and one-third in the cocoa. | Store in the refrigerator for up to 2 days.

peanut butter bites

Makes about 24 candies | Prep: 20 min + 3 hr to chill |
Level: 1

¾ cup (180 g) crunchy peanut butter
3 tablespoons confectioners' (icing) sugar
2 tablespoons unsweetened cocoa powder
4 oz (125 g) semisweet (dark) chocolate,
   melted
1 oz (30 g) white chocolate, melted

Beat the peanut butter, confectioners' sugar, and cocoa in a small bowl until well blended. Cover with aluminum foil and refrigerate until firm. | Form the mixture into a 10-inch (25-cm) roll and cut into 24 slices. | Transfer to a tray and freeze for 2 hours. | Dip each piece in semisweet chocolate and set at room temperature. | Drizzle with the white chocolate.

white chocolate and amaretti crunch

Makes 16–25 squares | Prep: 30 min + 4 hr to chill |
Level: 1

10 oz (300 g) white chocolate,
   coarsely chopped
⅔ cup (150 g) butter, cut up
4 tablespoons heavy (double) cream
3 oz (100 g) amaretti cookies, crushed
2 tablespoons shredded (desiccated) coconut
1 cup (100 g) chopped candied cherries
½ cup (50 g) flaked almonds, toasted

Line an 8-inch (20-cm) baking pan with parchment paper. | Melt the white chocolate and butter with the cream in a double boiler over barely simmering water. | Mix in the amaretti cookies, coconut, cherries, and almonds until well coated. | Spoon into the prepared pan, spreading it evenly. | Refrigerate for 4 hours, or until set. | Cut into squares.

hazelnut apricot truffles

Makes about 45 truffles | Prep: 20 min + overnight to chill the truffles | Cooking: 10 min | Level: 1

1 cup (200 g) superfine (caster) sugar
1 cup (250 ml) water
3 cups (300 g) finely ground hazelnuts
1 cup (100 g) chopped candied apricots
1/3 cup (50 g) unsweetened cocoa powder
1 tablespoon fresh lime juice
1 cup (150 g) confectioners' (icing) sugar
14 oz (400 g) semisweet (dark) chocolate, melted
1/2 cup (50 g) chopped candied apricots, extra
12 oz (300 g) semisweet (dark) chocolate, melted, extra

Truffles will keep, covered, in refrigerator for several weeks. This recipe is unsuitable to freeze or microwave. Cook the sugar and water in a medium saucepan over low heat, stirring constantly, until sugar has dissolved. Bring to a boil and boil for 5 minutes without stirring. Remove from the heat. | Mix in the nuts, apricots, cocoa, and lime juice. Cook over low heat for about 2 minutes, or until the mixture begins to thicken. | Stir in the confectioners' sugar and chocolate. | Set aside to cool to room temperature. | Roll level teaspoons of the mixture into balls around pieces of candied apricot. | Refrigerate overnight. | Dip the truffles in the extra chocolate and set at room temperature.

white chocolate almond bites

Makes 18 candies | Prep: 20 min + 1 hr to chill | Level: 1

7 oz (200 g) white chocolate, coarsely chopped
3/4 cup (180 g) butter
2 tablespoons corn (golden) syrup
2 tablespoons heavy (double) cream
8 oz (250 g) vanilla cookie crumbs
2 cups (200 g) chopped almonds
2/3 cup (90 g) flaked coconut, chopped
1 tablespoon Grand Marnier

For the Topping
5 oz (150 g) white chocolate
1 tablespoon butter

Line a 11 x 7-inch (28 x 18-cm) baking pan with waxed paper. Butter the paper. | Melt the chocolate and butter with the corn syrup and cream in a large saucepan over low heat, stirring constantly. | Stir in the cookie crumbs, almonds, coconut, and Grand Marnier. | Press the mixture into the prepared pan. | **Topping:** Melt the chocolate and butter in a double boiler over barely simmering water. Stir until smooth and spreadable. | Spread the topping over the mixture. Refrigerate for 1 hour, or until set. | Cut into squares.

chocolate ginger and almond dates

Makes about 30 candies | Prep: 20 min + 45 min to chill | Cooking: 5 min | Level: 1

13 oz (375 g) dates
6 tablespoons butter, melted
1 cup (100 g) flaked almonds
2 tablespoons superfine (caster) sugar
2 teaspoons amaretto
1 tablespoon chopped crystallized ginger
7 oz (200 g) semisweet (dark) chocolate

Carefully remove the pits from the dates. | Melt 4 tablespoons of butter in a large frying pan over medium heat. Add the almonds and sauté until lightly browned. | Process the almonds, sugar, liqueur, and ginger in a food processor or blender until smooth. | Fill the dates with the almond mixture. Refrigerate for 15 minutes. | Melt the chocolate with the remaining butter in a double boiler over barely simmering water. Dip the dates into the chocolate mixture. | Refrigerate for about 30 minutes, or until set. | Slice the dates before serving.

exotic fruit milk chocolate yums

Makes 40 candies | Prep: 20 min + 12 hr to macerate the pineapple + 1 hr to chill | Level: 1

3 rings crystallized pineapple, finely chopped
2 tablespoons Grand Marnier
½ cup (125 ml) heavy (double) cream
8 oz (250 g) milk chocolate, coarsely chopped
1 cup (100 g) chopped macadamia nuts

Macerate the pineapple in the liqueur in a small bowl overnight. | Bring the cream to a boil in a small saucepan. Add the chocolate and stir until melted and smooth. | Mix in the pineapple and liqueur. | Refrigerate for at least 1 hour, or until firm. | Form teaspoonfuls of the mixture into balls and roll in the nuts.

rocky roads

Makes 18–20 candies | Prep: 20 min + 90 min to chill and set | Level: 1

5 oz (150 g) white chocolate,
    coarsely chopped
2 tablespoons lightly crushed vanilla wafers
½ cup (50 g) coarsely chopped pecans
½ cup (50 g) coarsely chopped dried apricots
½ cup (60 g) mini marshmallows
4 candied cherries, coarsely chopped
3 oz (90 g) semisweet (dark) chocolate,
    coarsely chopped
Silver balls or sugar strands, jimmies, sprills,
    or sprinkles, to decorate

Line a cookie sheet with waxed paper. | Melt the white chocolate in a double boiler over barely simmering water. | Remove from the heat and mix in the vanilla wafers, pecans, apricots, marshmallows, and candied cherries until well coated. | Drop heaped tablespoons onto the cookie sheet. | Refrigerate for 1 hour, or until set. | Melt the semisweet chocolate in a double boiler over barely simmering water. Remove from the heat and dip the cookies halfway into the semisweet chocolate. | Decorate with the silver balls or sprinkle with sugar strands. | Set at room temperature for 30 minutes.

chocolate marshmallow nut fudge

Makes 18 candies | Prep: 20 min + 1 hr to chill | Level: 1

3½ oz (100 g) white marshmallows
3½ oz (100 g) pink marshmallows
4 tablespoons butter
1 tablespoon heavy (double) cream
4 oz (125 g) semisweet (dark) chocolate,
    coarsely chopped
1 teaspoon vanilla extract (essence)
1 cup (100 g) chopped macadamia nuts

Line an 11 x 7-inch (28 x 18-cm) baking pan with aluminum foil. | Mix the marshmallows, butter, and cream in a medium saucepan. Stir constantly over low heat until the marshmallows have melted. | Remove from the heat. Add the chocolate and vanilla and stir until the chocolate has melted. Beat for 1 minute and add the nuts. | Pour the mixture into the prepared pan. Refrigerate until set before cutting.

coffee slims

Makes 24 candies | Prep: 20 min + 1 hr to chill | Level: 1

8 oz (250 g) semisweet (dark) chocolate
4 tablespoons butter, melted
1 teaspoon instant coffee granules
2 tablespoons coffee liqueur

Butter a 8-inch (20-cm) square cake pan. Line with aluminum foil. | Melt the chocolate and butter with the coffee and liqueur in a double boiler over barely simmering water. Stir until smooth. | Pour into the prepared pan. Cover with foil and refrigerate until set. | Cut into triangles. Refrigerate before serving.

chocolate mint fudge

Makes 18 candies | Prep: 20 min + 1 hr to chill | Level: 1

1 lb (500 g) semisweet (dark) chocolate,
  coarsely chopped
1⅔ cups (400 ml) sweetened condensed milk
4 tablespoons butter
1 teaspoon mint extract (essence)
3½ oz (100 g) milk chocolate, melted

Line an 11 x 7-inch (28 x 18-cm) baking pan with aluminum foil. | Melt the semisweet chocolate with the condensed milk and butter in a large saucepan over low heat, stirring constantly, until smooth. | Add the mint extract. | Pour the mixture evenly into the prepared pan. | Refrigerate until set before cutting. | Drizzle with the milk chocolate and refrigerate until set.

cherry liqueur delights

Makes 30 candies | Prep: 20 min + overnight to macerate the cherries | Level: 1

15 candied cherries, halved
5 tablespoons cherry brandy
8 oz (250 g) semisweet (dark) chocolate

Macerate the cherries in the brandy in a small bowl overnight. | Drain the cherries, reserving the brandy. | Melt the chocolate with the brandy in a double boiler over barely simmering water until smooth. | Spoon a small amount of chocolate into foil petit-four cases. Place a half-cherry in each case and top with enough chocolate to fill the cases.

Sauces and Frostings

"Always serve too much hot fudge sauce on hot fudge sundaes.
It makes people overjoyed, and puts them in your debt."
Judith Olney

chocolate ganache

Makes 2 cups (500 ml) | Preparation: 20 min | Cooking: 5 min | Level: 1

1½ cups (375 ml) heavy (double) cream
1 tablespoon light corn (golden) syrup
10 oz (300 g) bittersweet (plain) chocolate, coarsely chopped

Great for filling mini meringues or spicing up mini muffins and a range of plain cakes.

Bring the cream and corn syrup to a boil in a medium saucepan over medium heat. Stir in the chocolate and set aside for 2 minutes. | Beat until the chocolate has melted and the mixture has thickened.

glossy chocolate frosting

Makes about 2½ cups (625 ml) | Prep: 15 min | Cooking: 10 min | Level: 1

6 oz (180 g) bittersweet (dark) chocolate
2 cups (300 g) confectioners' (icing) sugar
5 tablespoons boiling water
6 large egg yolks
½ cup (125 g) butter, softened

For a sparkling (and expensive) finish to the most stylish of desserts, swirl in a sachet of gold dust.

Melt the chocolate in a double boiler over barely simmering water. | Beat in ½ cup (75 g) of confectioners' sugar and the water until well blended. | Beat the egg yolks with the remaining confectioners' sugar in a saucepan until blended. Cook over low heat, stirring constantly, until the mixture registers 160°F (71°C) on an instant-read thermometer. Beat in the chocolate mixture and butter until well blended. | Plunge the pan into a bowl of ice water. Stir until cooled.

simple chocolate frosting

Makes about 1½ cups (375 ml) | Prep: 10 min | Level: 1

2 cups (300 g) confectioners' sugar
⅓ cup (50 g unsweetened cocoa powder
2 tablespoons butter
1 teaspoon vanilla extract (essence)
About 2 tablespoons boiling water

Stir together the confectioners' sugar, cocoa, and butter in a medium bowl. Add the vanilla and enough of the boiling water to obtain a firm paste. | Stir until soft and spreadable.

white chocolate ganache

Makes about 1½ cups (375 ml) | Prep: 15 min + 30 min to chill | Cooking: 5 min | Level: 1

½ cup (125 ml) heavy (double) cream
12 oz (300 g) white chocolate,
  coarsely chopped

Heat the cream almost to a boil in a small saucepan over low heat. | Place the chocolate in a large bowl. | Pour the cream over the chocolate and stir until the chocolate is melted and smooth. | Refrigerate until thickened and spreadable, about 30 minutes, stirring occasionally.

chocolate walnut frosting

Makes 2 cups (500 ml) | Prep: 10 min | Level: 1

4 oz (125 g) semisweet (dark) chocolate,
  coarsely chopped
6 tablespoons butter, cut up
2½ cups (375 g) confectioners' (icing) sugar
1 teaspoon vanilla extract (essence)
1 tablespoon fresh lemon juice
1 cup (100 g) coarsely chopped walnuts

Melt the chocolate and butter in a double boiler over barely simmering water. Set aside to cool. | Beat in the confectioners' sugar, vanilla, and lemon juice. Add the walnuts. Use immediately.

chocolate sour cream frosting

Makes 2½ cups (625 ml) | Prep: 15 min + 5 min to cool | Level: 1

8 oz (250 g) semisweet (dark) chocolate,
  coarsely chopped
4 tablespoons butter, softened
½ cup (125 ml) sour cream
2⅔ cups (400 g) confectioners' (icing) sugar

Melt the chocolate in a double boiler over barely simmering water. | Add the butter and cool for 5 minutes. | Stir in the sour cream. Beat in the confectioners' sugar until smooth and spreadable.

gooey fudge sauce with almonds and raspberries

Makes about 1½ cups (375 ml) | Prep: 15 min | Cooking: 25 min | Level: 1

5 oz (150 g) bittersweet (dark) chocolate, coarsely chopped
½ cup (125 g) butter, cut up
2½ cups (500 g) superfine (caster) sugar
1½ cups (325 ml) sweetened condensed milk
Pinch of salt
1 teaspoon vanilla extract (essence)
Slivered almonds, raspberries, and vanilla ice cream, to serve

Melt the chocolate with the butter in a double boiler over barely simmering water. | Pour into a saucepan and stir in the sugar, condensed milk, and salt. | Cook over medium heat for 20-25 minutes, or until thickened. | Add the vanilla and remove from the heat. | Pour the sauce over ice cream and decorate with almonds and raspberries.

chocolate pastry cream

Makes about 2½ cups (625 ml) | Prep: 15 min | Cooking: 15 min | Level: 1

5 large egg yolks
2/3 cup (120 g) granulated sugar
1/3 cup (50 g) all-purpose (plain) flour
2 cups (500 ml) milk
Pinch of salt
1/2 teaspoon vanilla extract (essence)
7 oz (200 g) bittersweet (dark) chocolate, coarsely chopped

This classic custard can be used to fill cakes and meringues, or serve it on its own with some fresh berry fruit and whipped cream.

Beat the egg yolks and sugar in a large bowl until pale and thick. | Bring the milk to a boil with the salt and vanilla, then stir it into the egg and sugar. | Cook over low heat, stirring constantly with a wooden spoon, until the mixture thickens and lightly coats the back of a metal spoon. | Gradually add the chocolate, stirring until it has dissolved into the cream. Remove from the heat.

Index

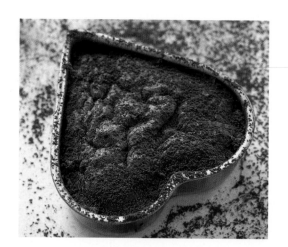